Henry Conrad

# Morality
# and the
# Homosexual

# Morality
# and the
# Homosexual

A CATHOLIC APPROACH TO A MORAL PROBLEM

by

## Rev. Michael J. Buckley, D.D.

With Foreword by
MOST REV. JOHN C. HEENAN, D.D.
Archbishop of Liverpool

## THE NEWMAN PRESS
Westminster, Maryland

*First American printing, 1960*

*Nihil obstat:* JOANNES DINN, S.T.D.
    *Censor deputatus*

*Imprimatur:* ✝ GEORGIUS PATRICIUS,
    EPUS. LOIDENSIS.

*die 22a Octobris 1959*

Library of Congress Catalog Card No. 59–14804

© SANDS & CO (PUBLISHERS) LTD
15 King St, London, W.C.2

# Introduction

~~~~~~~~~~~~~~~~~~~~~~~~~~~~~~~~~~~~~~~~~~~~~~

THE complex subject of homosexuality in its wider aspects receives far too little attention in Catholic manuals and text-books of moral and pastoral theology, and the treatment which it receives is usually considered in terms of acts rather than of condition. Such treatment is inadequate for the conscientious and sympathetic priest, who wishes to try to help his homosexual subjects through a deeper understanding of the causes and nature of their psycho-sexual disorder which gives rise to these unnatural sinful acts. In other fields the priest is better served; there is, for instance, a considerable literature by Catholics or acceptable to Catholics on the nature and causes of alcoholic and narcotic addiction from the medical and psychological point of view, which a confessor would naturally consult in dealing with a chronic dypsomaniac or drug addict. But there is little guidance for his dealings with the homosexual.

Even were this sexual anomaly a rarity the situation would be serious enough, but unhappily recent publicity has emphasized its prevalence, and probably an increasing prevalence, in England today. Priests who work in large cities are becoming increasingly aware of this. The reasons for such an increase in incidence do not come within the scope of this book except in so far as certain factors of environment may be a contributary cause, such

as the segregation of the sexes in the armed services during times of war.  Nor is this book concerned with the
relative incidence of the anomaly among different races
and nations, or the reasons for its alleged prevalence
among Anglo-Saxon, Teutonic and Nordic peoples more
than among those of Latin or Celtic stock.  Nor do we
consider it in terms of a possible aspect of national decadence, as suggested by the history of past civilizations.
Clearly it would be impossible to study every aspect of
this complex and highly controversial subject in a single
volume.  The scope of this book is confined to what we
consider most urgent and necessary at the present time—
a thorough moral evaluation of the problem, and a purely
pastoral approach to its solution as it arises in the
penitent.

A comparatively brief scientific examination is included of the medical, hereditary, environmental and
psychological factors which are claimed to explain why
certain people are psycho-sexually attracted to their own
sex, and yield to these impulses by engaging in homosexual acts.  Thus it is hoped that the priest will be
assisted in his pastoral ministrations, particularly in the
confessional, and may be helped in his attempts to estimate the degree of responsibility in those concerned.
There are non-Catholic psychologists who approach the
problem too emotionally and subjectively, even to the
extent of condoning homosexual acts, in a misplaced
sympathy for the patient's condition for which he may
not be wholly responsible.  On the other hand, there are
Catholic priests who judge purely by the act, on a rule-of-
thumb basis, without paying any attention to the deep-
seated disorientation of the homosexual pattern which

gives rise to the act, and thus fail to get to the root of the problem, or bring about a sound amendment of life.

The priest who has time only to dabble superficially in the medical and psychological literature on the subject may well find himself more confused than enlightened by a bewildering conflict of evidence and terminology. The very word 'homosexual' is ambiguous; in popular parlance, and in a good deal of literature as well, it is applied to those who actually indulge in homosexual acts. Others apply the term to those whose inclinations are directed more or less exclusively towards their own sex even though their impulses may be as thoroughly controlled as those of the 'normal' celibate. There are authors who specify the latter category of homosexuals as 'inverts' or 'Uranians' to distinguish them from the 'practising' homosexual.

There is a confusing jargon of terms to describe the various intermediate stages between homosexuality and heterosexuality. Various types of homosexuals are distinguished according to their sexual acts, whether 'active' and masculine or 'passive' and feminine, and so on. This confusion of terms, and the indiscriminate use made of certain of them, can lead to false conclusions. Therefore it is necessary at the start to establish a strict terminology which will be used throughout this book. It is of paramount importance to distinguish between the homosexual condition and homosexual acts.

If it were to be proved that in some cases at least the condition is congenital, then the person concerned is clearly not morally responsible for the direction of his sexual instincts. This would apply also to those cases where it appears certain that the condition arose from unfortunate incidents of corruption or assault, forced on a boy at or just before puberty, which warped his subsequent inclinations. It would of course be utterly destructive of the objective basis of Catholic moral theology to hold that people in these conditions are automatically exonerated from all responsibility and blame for their homosexual acts. On the other hand, it is lacking in reality and even justice to judge such acts out of the context of the conditions as sheer wilful unprovoked perverseness.

Even though it has never been proved that the homosexual finds it physically more difficult to control his impulses than the heterosexual, nevertheless many other peculiar factors enter in at this point. Strong social taboos and in some countries a stern penal code, as well as moral principles and personal fastidiousness may restrain him. He is not susceptible to the constant barrage of sex stimulation provided by the dance hall, the salacious magazine or certain newspapers, the cinema and music-hall, and even by much commercial advertising. The biggest difficulty, however, which confronts the homosexual who desires to lead a life of chastity is the fact that he lives in an environment of his own sex with all the inevitable intimacies. Unfortunately it must be admitted that in the past few years a new type of illustrated literature has grown up which caters for his homosexual inclinations, and whereas thirty years ago *The Well of Loneliness* was banned in England amidst an outcry of public indignation, many far more blatant and outspoken novels on homosexual themes have appeared since almost without comment. Just as in heterosexual matters, these factors must be taken into account in assessing the prevalence of the anomaly and the degree of responsibility that must be attributed to those who are homosexually inclined, or engage in homosexual practices.

The first chapter of this book, therefore, is concerned with the establishment of a precise terminology which will then be used throughout in order to avoid false conclusions and misunderstandings, for as we have already seen, even the term 'homosexual' is a wide one. With the help of this terminology we hope to assist the priest in adopting an attitude to the problem that is in accordance with justice and reality, and with the principles of Catholic moral theology.

We will also attempt in the following chapter to estimate the extent of homosexuality in England by applying our terminology to the available statistics. This is not an easy task, and anything approaching a precise result is clearly impossible. Statistics are based mainy on police-court and criminal proceedings, and to a lesser extent on what doctors and psychologists are willing to disclose about their patients. Those of homosexual disposition who have their impulse under perfect control will clearly never become involved in the former, and rarely in the latter category. Furthermore, it is generally admitted, and recently in the *Wolfenden Report*, that the great majority even of 'practising' homosexuals never fall foul of the police, particularly where both parties to an act are consenting adults. Most of them manage their affairs with sufficient discretion and reticence to escape detection, and in practice the British police concern themselves mainly with flagrant violations of public decency and the corruption of minors rather than with private immoralities which do not obtrude themselves on their notice. Again doctors and psychologists are sometimes consulted only when an arrest is feared to be imminent, for many judges are known to take a more lenient view if the culprit can claim to be already under medical or psychiatric treatment.

The next section is concerned with the etiological factors involved, for on these depends the subjective morality of homosexuality. Our examination of the medical and psychological theories will be largely based on the *Report submitted by the British Medical Association to the Wolfenden Committee*, for this Report represents the most recent finding of present day medical and psychiatric knowledge as to the cause of homosexuality, and enumerates the most outstanding contributions to this subject. The Wolfenden Committee, however, was concerned, not with the subjective or objective morality of homosexuality, nor with its causes or cure, but with proposed changes in the penal code and dealt with as a social Report. But the Report is also useful in forming an evaluation of the case for the constitutional character of homosexuality.

Following the medical and physiological approach to the problem, the next section is devoted to an outline and examination of four main schools of thought which seek to explain homosexuality on a psychological basis; namely, Freud, Adler, Jung and Gide. It is clearly impossible in the scope of this book to examine all the ramifications of their various theories in great detail, but a brief appreciation of their contributions will help to explain the true nature of the problem. This book, we must stress, is mainly concerned with a pastoral approach to homosexuality, and therefore the environmental factor is particularly examined as more clearly relevant.

Environment is considered under two headings. First, the family, and, second, society in general. First, the family background, which is usually considered the most important of all. Some psychological theories attribute homosexuality to a mother-fixation (or father-fixation in the case of the Lesbian or female homosexual) which may be accompanied by a feeling of perhaps subconscious hostility to the other parent, even in very early childhood. Again, many case-histories suggest that the homosexual often comes from a broken or unhappy home, in which case a latent distaste for marriage, and consequently for the normal sexual act, may be subconsciously instilled even at an early age. In the social scale it has been tentatively alleged by some that homosexuality occurs most frequently in the upper classes and in the working classes, but less so among the middle class. This may be because the bourgeoisie in England are on the whole more stable and normal in their marriage and family life than the aristocracy or the proletariat. Evidence on the social incidence of the problem is so conflicting and contradictory, however, that we have not considered it worth while or relevant to take it into consideration.

Then, we will go on to consider the wider society outside the family circle in our examination of environmental factors, with a study of the effects of sex-segregation on the adolescent and adult homosexual. The English public school system has received a good deal of blame in this matter, and in this century received some publicity through such novels as Compton Mackenzie's *Sinister Street* and C. S. Lewis's *Surprised by Joy*. This segregation usually occurs during a boy's most critical and formative years, immediately preceding, during, and immediately after puberty—a stage of development which has powerful psychological as well as physical aspects. Reliable evidence from this source can only come from the boys themselves in later years, for again most incidents do not come to the attention of the masters. This evidence, however, is often conflicting. The 'good' boy of stable character and sound morals may himself be quite unaware of what is going on among his more dissolute schoolmates, who will instinctively avoid him in even discussing such topics. There are a few co-educational boarding-schools which claim that, despite the obvious risks of 'natural' immorality their moral tone is far higher than in segregated boarding-schools, and that homosexual offences are almost unknown there, but there is insufficient evidence to establish this. Such institutions are not very numerous in England, and there is strong prejudice against them.

The next problem of segregation is presented by the armed forces—for English universities, even the older ones of Oxford and Cambridge, have largely lost any character of segregation. In the armed services there is clearly a less close surveillance of personal habits and morals than in the boarding school, and therefore there is usually no lack of opportunity for homosexual acts. The Navy in particular has been singled out for blame in some circles, partly because during long exercises afloat the segregation is more complete, but it is doubtful whether statistics can be made to support a higher incidence of homosexuality here than in the Army or Air Force. It is possible, however, that this tradition in itself attracts the already-formed homosexual into the Navy in cases where he has a choice of services.

By the time the young man enters the armed services, however, it is generally agreed that his sexual orientation is more or less permanently fixed. A healthy heterosexual youth who leaves the services with homosexual habits has therefore acquired them fairly late in life, either through curiosity (which may happen at any age) or simply as a substitute, perhaps reluctant and even distasteful at first, for normal sexual relations. From a pastoral point of view it is usually urged that cures are much easier to effect in such cases than when the disorientation occurs at an earlier age and seems to form a more integral part of the person's make-up.

Another form of segregation in abnormal cases is prison, where most authorities agree that homosexual acts, if only as a substitute, are rife. Certainly those convicted of homosexual offences are unlikely to find their condition in any way improved as a result of a prison sentence, and medical and psychiatric facilities for treatment of it in British prisons are far from adequate.

After this examination of causality, the next chapter presents an examination of the objective morality of homosexuality. Biblical and Patristic sources, as well as the Penitentials and the Natural Law, form the starting points. These sources, however, are concerned chiefly with the sinful nature of homosexual acts, and there is little or no consideration in them of our problem as a condition. In the Old Testament we are presented with the history of Sodom and the terrible vengeance that fell upon that city. The 'Sin of Sodom' has become identified in the popular mind and in most moral text-books with certain homosexual practices. Certainly the Levitical law took an extremely grave view of such acts, and the Prophets thundered the wrath of God against these abominations. There is no explicit reference to homosexual practices in the Gospels, except possibly in the passage where Our Lord declares that the sins of the Pharisees and Scribes would be judged more severely than those of Sodom and Gomorrah, which is in keeping with His frequent emphasis on the fact that the sins of the spirit may be a species more grave than the sins of the flesh. St. Paul, however, returns to the language of the Prophets in his denunciation of unnatural acts.

In the light of present day investigations, which we have examined, we can attempt to lay down principles on the basis of which the individual's responsibility for his condition and practices can be determined. For pastoral purposes the dispositions of homosexuals may be classified under three headings: those who are troubled in conscience and beset by shame and self-loathing and who are genuinely striving after sexual normality; those who objectively realize the obligation of making such an effort but are reluctant and frightened to make the attempt of changing something they feel integral to their personalities; and those who disregard the moral law entirely as something quite irrelevant to their own condition, and continue in their homosexual habits. Normally the priest will see little of this last category in his confessional; if they are Catholics at all they will presumably have lapsed altogether from the Sacraments. But the second category, in common with the third, is capable of putting up a specious and emotional barrier of self-defence in the subjective sphere, arguing that the category of sins against nature does not apply to people in his condition because, he will say, homosexual acts are not contrary to *his* nature but in accordance with it.  He may say, too, that the Church counsels matrimony as the normal state of life for the average man or woman who has no vocation to celibacy, but has no answer for the homosexual who may similarly have no such vocation. In this context it should be borne in mind that we condemn any religious bodies, as well as individual moralists, who in defending the practice of contraception by confusing the purposes of matrimony, put sexual fulfilment and mutual help and companionship on an equality with the primary purpose of procreation. Such views play into the hands of homosexuals.  If sexual pleasure and companionship are regarded as equally primary, and if procreation may be legitimately prevented by artificial means, the force of the argument against homosexual unions where there is genuine affection is enormously weakened. Homosexuals who are prone to self-justification in specious home-made moral codes are quick to seize upon this point and make the most of it.  The findings of the Lambeth Conference of 1958 are certainly not helpful in this respect.

Sometimes in a spirit of arrogance, sometimes in self-pity, the homosexual may try to claim himself to be an exception and exempt from the moral law in this respect. The priest should be knowledgeable and alert in dealing with this type of subjective defence-mechanism and fallacious rationalization.  Accordingly, in this book, the priest's role is outlined, his attitude to the homosexual discussed, and the relationship which should exist between himself, the doctor and the psychiatrist in the treatment of the homosexual is also considered.

The vocational guidance which should be given to

homosexuals is a matter of great importance, and will vary greatly according to the individual, his circumstances, capacities, inclinations, aptitudes, and actual or potential powers of self-control. Some occupations are unsuitable and dangerous, others may with safety give special scope to their particular temperament, and homosexuals may use them for the glory of God and the benefit of society. The possibility and advisability of entering the married state must be considered together with the dangers of recommending this too indiscriminately as a cure. We will consider also the problem of whether vocations to the religious life should be encouraged among them, whether a controlled homosexual disposition can be compatible with the sacerdotal state, bearing in mind that a certain type of superficial religiosity, which may be mistaken in its early stages for a vocation, is often to be found in the adolescent homosexual. In this way, then, we hope that this book will provide practical pastoral guidance at all relevant points to the priest and confessor in his dealings with the homosexual problem, and be of some help in evaluating both the guilt and the degree of responsibility in his homosexual subjects.

# Contents

# Foreword

~~~~~~~~~~~~~~~~~~~~~~~~~~~~~~~~~~~~~~~~~~~~~~~~~

IT would be trite to call the appearance of this book
timely, since a pastoral guide to the treatment of the homosexual is so obviously urgent and indispensable. Most
priests have been canvassed for their views on the Wolfenden Report and the treatment of homosexual behaviour
must have become a practical problem for many confessors. This book is concerned only incidentally to provide the priest with well-informed comment on the Report.
Its chief and admirable purpose is to show him how to
help penitents tempted to commit homosexual sins.

Without expert guidance the priest may harm sensitive
souls and for a variety of reasons homosexuals are usually
most sensitive souls. In order to help them the priest does
not need to set himself up as an amateur psychiatrist. It is
true that the reputation of professionals in the field is not
unduly high. For this there is a double explanation. In the
first place, as a science psychiatry is still young and will
always be inexact. Medical men often tend, rather un-
fairly, to sneer at their colleagues who practise psychiatry.
They may disparage them by the sobriquet "trick
cyclists". Yet most of us gratefully seek the services of a
sound psychiatrist when we have to deal with maladjusted
people.

Psychiatrists, moreover, suffer loss of prestige from the
brash assertions of those practitioners who always seem

available to argue for the defence in criminal cases. When barristers, without any deep psychological knowledge, make expert witnesses sound absurd, the whole profession suffers. Small wonder if some priests dismiss psychiatry as nonsense and prefer to use what they describe as robust common sense in dealing with the aberrations of their penitents.

But robust common sense is not enough. Without yielding to the temptation of posing as psychologists, confessors need to know enough about psychology to be able to judge when a penitent should become a patient. The confessor ought to know when and if to recommend penitents to consult a doctor.

This book may not win the approval of those doctors and lawyers who style themselves progressive. The important point is that it was written for neither. Essentially it is a contribution to pastoral theology. We are told what attitude to take and what treatment to give to homosexuals who come to consult us or seek direction in the sacrament of penance.

Dr. Buckley's book does not pretend to be a substitute for manuals of moral theology. The general principles learned during the seminary course remain valid whatever new problem the casuist has to face. But there are fashions in behaviour as in clothes. There are even fashions in sinful behaviour. What in one generation incurs ostracism invites only mild rebuke or even tolerance in the next. It is not long since being divorced carried a social stigma. Today it is no longer a bar to receiving a knighthood. I do not suggest that the modern attitude is necessarily wrong. But it is certainly significant. Some claim that precisely because we have become more tolerant in our attitude towards sinners we have become more Christian. But it can equally well be argued that we are more tolerant only because we have become less Christian and therefore less shocked by sin. For our present purpose it is enough to observe that moral standards alter. There can be no doubt that homosexuality presents a special problem to the priests of this generation.

The case of Oscar Wilde was so singular as not to disturb Catholic moralists. In the social climate of those days it gave general satisfaction that unnatural and detestable vice had been awarded condign punishment. There was no call for research by theologians.

The outlook has changed. Nobody today would pretend that the only treatment needed by homosexuals is a term of imprisonment. We may now have more Oscar Wildes or perhaps homosexual behaviour is not more widespread but only more flagrant. Whatever the reasons, public opinion has changed. Apart from the question of whether or not consenting males who indulge in homosexual acts should be treated as criminals, the fact is that such behaviour would once have evoked universal disgust. In some quarters it now attracts only sympathy.

This change of views affects the pastoral work of the priest. Subjects traditionally regarded as unmentionable are now discussed without shame even by the young. People once condemned without pity are recognized to be in need of help. To some extent the modern attitude arises from lack of the sense of sin. Without condoning this error we have to admit that the man who commits sin with one of his own sex is not necessarily a worse type than the adulterer who breaks up a family. In the sight of God his personal guilt may be less. Moral theology is more than a mere listing of sins according to their degrees of gravity. Unnatural vice is more heinous than some other sins, but the sinner need not be further from forgiveness. Until we know the extent of his culpability we cannot place the sinner in a category. This we can do only with sins.

Yet it is wise for priests to be on their guard against the views of some modern champions of penal reform. These tend to adopt a soft approach which has nothing in common with Christian compassion for sinners. There is a school of reform which would abolish the very notion of sin. A delinquent is mentally sick. Underlying the recommendations of such reformers is the philosophy of determinism. They contend that criminals are victims of their impulses and environment. It is true that imputability must be measured by the physical, psychological and social condition of the law-breaker. But any system which refuses to consider free will and grace as realities is fundamentally in error.

For this reason the appearance of *Morality and the Homosexual* is opportune. Due consideration is given to the causes of homosexual tendencies. But Dr. Buckley never loses sight of the fact that the homosexual is a man enjoying freedom and capable of being sustained by the grace of God.

Priests who may have thought homosexuals to be beyond hope of reform will be heartened by what they read. They will learn—what Catholic psychiatrists have already discovered—that a patient confessor can succeed where others have failed. One reason is that the priest is bound to be an optimist. He will approach his problem in the spirit of Christian hope while refusing to admit that there can ever be a hopeless case. For there is no limit to the mercy and power of God.

The priest, says Dr. Buckley, must break the fatalism which usually obsesses the homosexual. Who, better than the priest, is able to break fatalism? Every priest of experience knows that God still works miracles of grace in the souls of sinners. A careful reading of this book will enable the pastor of souls to co-operate more fully with the delicate operations of the Divine Physician.

✝ JOHN C. HEENAN,
*Archbishop of Liverpool.*

*Whit Sunday,* 1959.

# Acknowledgments

~~~~~~~~~~~~~~~~~~~~~~~~~~~~~~~~~~~~~~~~~~~~~~~~~

GRATEFUL acknowledgment is made to the following, who have kindly granted permission to quote extracts from their printed works: Messrs. Burns Oates & Washbourne Ltd., for permission to quote from *Sex Enlightenment*, by Fr. L. S. J. King. Messrs. Victor Gollancz Ltd., *Society and the Homosexual*, by G. W. Westwood. The Mercier Press Ltd., *New Problems in Medical Ethics*, by Pere Charles Larere, edited by Dom Peter Flood. Messrs. William Heinemann Ltd., *They Stand Apart*, edited by Judge Tudor Rees and Harley V. Usill; *The Psychology of Sex*, by Havelock Ellis, the latter being published by Heinemann Medical Books Ltd. Messrs. Bailliere, Tindall & Cox Ltd., *The Invert*, by Anomaly. *The Lancet* and *The Practitioner* for permission to quote short extracts. Finally grateful acknowledgment is made to the British Medical Association for permission to quote from their report on *Homosexuality and Prostitution*.

# CHAPTER ONE

# The Terminology and Nature of Homosexuality

THE Wolfenden Report clearly demonstrated the considerable attention which has been focused in recent times on the problem of homosexuality. There is a strong human tendency to approach major sexual problems with violent emotional prejudice, and homosexuality is no exception. Homosexual practices have been known throughout the centuries, and the decline of some great nations of antiquity is generally attributed to this cause. For many who claim to speak with authority on the subject widespread indulgence in homosexual acts is the inevitable accompanying sign of a nation's decadence and fall from power. The passage of time, however, has not brought a solution. Rather has it brought a riot of conflicting opinions which reflect personal bias rather than true statement of fact. It is necessary, therefore, to examine the available scientific evidence in order to establish objectively the causality, frequency and extent of this sexual anomaly.

Such evidence is scanty and reasons are not difficult to find. The homosexual, as a rule, is secretive about his sexual life. But even when no overt acts have taken place, to be branded as a homosexual is probably, among ordinary men, the worst stigma that can affect anyone, and some homosexuals are said to have committed suicide because of society's attitude towards them.   Whether or not such a stigma is merited will depend upon his responsibility for his sexual condition.   If this is congenital, then he is not guilty of moral reproach, just as a blind man is not condemned by society because of his blindness.

The word homosexual generally conjures up an image of a depraved, sensual, lustful maniac from whom there is nothing but revulsion.   This concept of the homosexual is held by some who have made a special study of the problem, while others, no less qualified, consider him the unfortunate, helpless victim of a cruel twist of fate.   They demand a 'new moral code' by which he can express himself sexually in the only medium available to him—the homosexual.[1]   The difficulty of sifting the truth from the prolific writings of these diametrically opposed views is increased by the dearth of Catholic literature on the subject.   The homosexual may be innocent or guilty of his condition, yet it is the duty of the moralist to safeguard any redress which society may deem fit to take at the expense of the moral law.

There are many who hold that homosexuality is so rare that it does not merit the attention given to it and that sexual anomalies are best left undiscussed.   Ignoring for the moment the question whether homosexuality is a disease, it may help to draw a parallel between it and the vast amount of medical research that is undertaken in

---

[1] " It would be much more sensible if society would take a boy as he is and fit a moral code to him instead of twisting him to comply with a predetermined sex code." *Society and the Homosexual*.  Gordon Westwood (London, 1952) p. 174.

order to diagnose some uncommon disease affecting a very small minority of the population. Yet is homosexuality so rare? On examination we find that homosexual practices are prevalent to such an extent that some claim it is one of the greatest emotional problems of modern times involving a vast number of people. The moralist attempts to examine every difficulty that may impinge on the salvation of a human soul and it is to this end that the present work on homosexuality is directed.

The discussion of sexual anomalies is best left to competent persons and should never become the topic of drawing-room conversation. Yet it is certainly true that the whole subject of homosexuality, like other sexual matters, is much more openly and freely discussed today than it was formerly. Public interest has increased, with the consequence that court cases are more frequently reported in the daily newspapers. Many serious articles have appeared in magazines and books which deal either entirely or incidentally with the problem. Yet the popular press is guilty on many occasions of treating the subject as sensational news value, ignoring completely its serious side. Again in the autumn of 1958 the Lord Chamberlain of England announced that serious plays on homosexual themes would be considered for licence in public theatres, whereas formerly such plays were confined to club theatres outside his jurisdiction. There are thinly veiled references to homosexual practices on stage, screen and television, and the subject is often introduced by way of innuendo or sneer. In such circumstances, silence is not golden where the moralist is concerned.

Society may condone or condemn if the right to do so is established. It should always condemn immoral sexual practices, and homosexual acts are included in this category. Yet if there be such a person as a congenital homosexual, then society should allow him to fulfil a useful purpose and not spurn him merely for what he is. If he turns to decent-living men and is rejected, then he may be driven to seek companionship where he can find it rather than where he would prefer. It is a small step to the homosexual level of the underworld where he will meet others similarly affected, and there is no need to stress the evil of such an environment. Many homosexual lapses are generally attributed to the homosexual's loneliness, and the homosexual may well be less worried about freedom to express himself physically than in the removal of this social obstacle to his acceptance as a man with a right to a place in society. If he is innocent, then he should receive the necessary encouragement from men inspired with Christian charity to enable him to fulfil the moral law. Here there should be no one better equipped to help him than a priest.

Many priests hold that homosexuality is a purely medical field into which they cannot and should not enter. They would leave the whole problem to the doctor or psychiatrist, and this practice has led in the past, and still leads, to disastrous results. Others condemn homosexuals out of hand without a hearing, while there are not a few who feel keenly their apparent inability to help someone who comes in desperation seeking their aid. Even were a case to arise where medical assistance must be sought, the supernatural destiny of the penitent must never be forgotten. The priest, the supernatural therapist, must guide the whole emotional structure of the confessed homosexual into selfless and positively constructive channels so that he may achieve his eternal salvation. Moral judgement must be passed not only on the homosexual, but also on the morality of any prescribed medical treatment. Indeed there are many doctors today who hold that the problem of homosexuality is essentially and predominantly of a moral nature.

The only evidence available to the investigator who endeavours to solve the question of what makes a man a homosexual is to be found in Police reports, official statistics, writings of homosexuals themselves, and in the testimony of priests, doctors, psychiatrists and all those who are in some way connected with the problem through their dealings with homosexuals. The grave danger is that a selective rather than a true cross-section of the homosexual world will influence any judgement that may be made. It is a characteristic of the homosexual not to seek advice unless he already finds himself in trouble with his moral conscience or with the laws of society.

Now we intend to make a scientific examination of the problem and such a study involves the use of certain words in a specifically technical sense. Clarity will suffer if such words are used indiscriminately, and it is obvious to all investigators of the question at issue that the already complex problem of homosexuality is rendered far more difficult by the careless use of terminology far removed from the meaning that it was originally intended to convey. The word *homosexuality* itself, for instance, is used equally haphazardly by men like Kinsey to denote either homosexual practices or a condition in which one is attracted to those of the same sex. This failure to make the distinction between the condition and homosexual practices conveys the impression that every homosexual engages in homosexual acts, and thus destroys the concept of a chaste homosexual. Indulgence in homosexual activity is, in fact, no more than an indication that the subject may be a homosexual, just as indulgence in heterosexual acts is not an infallible proof that the subject is not a homosexual. The grave danger in this problem is the approach from a purely statistical analysis of human behaviour, concluding from what a man does to what a man is, ignoring motive, circumstances and the other conditioning determinants of human actions.

A homosexual is called an 'invert' or 'pervert', the former conveying the impression that his anomaly is constitutional and morally irreprehensible, while the popular meaning of the word pervert implies someone who has deliberately turned away from what he once was, could be again if he liked, and in the opinion of the speaker should be.[2] These definitions cannot be accepted as they presuppose the proof which they require: namely, that the homosexual is or is not responsible for his homosexual condition. One cannot, for instance, be a pervert from something which one has never been.

The rabid supporters of a new moral code for the practising homosexual twist words at the expense of truth to

[2] "Some writers on the subject—have drawn a distinction between the 'invert' and the 'pervert'. We have not found this distinction useful. It suggests that it is possible to distinguish between two men who commit the same offence, the one as the result of his constitution, the other from a perverse and deliberate choice, with the further suggestion that the former is in some sense less culpable than the latter. To make this distinction as a matter of definition seems to prejudice a very difficult question." *Wolfenden Report*. (London, 1957) pp. 16-17.
'Anomaly' calls a homosexual by the term 'invert' and concludes: "To call inverts perverts is equivalent to calling them shameful and does, in fact, damn them out of hand." *The Invert*. 'Anomaly' (2nd Edit. London, 1948) p. 5.

suit their biassed views. 'Desire' becomes an 'irresistible impulse': 'inclination' is raised to the status of 'necessity' and 'normal' is claimed as 'natural'. Inaccurate use of these words, so vital to an understanding of the point to be solved, is reprehensible when used in everyday language: it is unforgivable when one finds it in the writings of those who claim to approach the problem from a purely scientific viewpoint.

With this in mind, the following terminology is submitted which will be used throughout this book. Homosexuality is a psychosexual attraction towards members of the same sex. It is a sexual bias or 'propensity' which constitutes the major sexual drive of the individual. The danger of defining homosexuality as a state or condition is that it may be immediately presumed that there is a parity between it and heterosexuality, and that homosexuals are born with this homosexual drive. The homosexual may use it as an argument to legitimize his way of 'making love' and presume that because he is different he has a right to a new moral code. If he also holds that the sexual urge must find expression, then he will claim that he has no control over, or responsibility for, his homosexual practices. Nevertheless, the distinction between the homosexual condition and homosexual acts is of supreme importance.

If the study of homosexuality were to be comprehensive then it should include the psychosexual attraction of women towards women, commonly called Lesbianism, but this book confines itself to the male's attraction towards his own sex. While it may be true that there are certain similarities in the homosexual pattern, whether male or female, nevertheless the different physical and psychological structural differences between the sexes would limit the number and validity of inferences which could be drawn from a common study.

Homosexuality is not an 'all or none' condition, and grave mistakes have been made by classifying men as one kind or the other with nothing in between.

"All graduations can exist—from apparently exclusive homosexuality without any conscious capacity for arousal by heterosexual stimuli, to apparently exclusive heterosexuality."[3]

While the psychoanalytical theory of the universality of the homosexual component in everybody is not accepted by us, yet the existence of the homosexual urge which varies quantitatively in certain persons must be admitted. This in turn can vary quantitatively in the same individual at different periods of his life. The existence of this sexual bias is shown by what is felt or from what is done by the persons concerned, but either method may lead to fallacious conclusions. An individual may be quite genuinely unaware of his homosexual propensities for many reasons: e.g. the weakness of the sexual urge, a satisfying vocation, religious standards or the reluctance to admit even to himself a sexual urge which is socially condemned.

On the other hand, many heterosexuals may engage in homosexual practices because of special circumstances such as the all-male environment in prisons and prisoner-of-war camps. It would be wrong to conclude from irregular behaviour in such abnormal surroundings that their conduct was due to the homosexual component in their make-up. Such a course would serve merely to tie a convenient tag on what may in reality be the expression

[3] *Wolfenden Report*, p. 12.

of the strength of the heterosexual urge which finds its outlet in the only available substitute-medium.

This homosexual bias can affect behaviour in a variety of ways, some of which are not obviously sexual, since

"it must not be thought that the existence of the homosexual propensity necessarily leads to homosexual behaviour of an overtly sexual kind ".[4]

Some homosexuals are quite unaware of the existence of the homosexual instinct within themselves, and their homosexuality is described as *latent*. Their homosexuality is inferred from their behaviour in non-sexual spheres. Although the extent and variety of behaviour which can be legitimately inferred as indicative of a homosexual propensity is grossly exaggerated, nevertheless such inferences can be drawn in certain cases. There are, for example, some occupations which call for devoted service to others, and latent homosexuality may provide the motivation and stimulus for such an undertaking. It would be contrary to fact to conceive homosexuality as necessarily evil in all its facets.

Since homosexual behaviour is not an infallible guide by itself alone as to whether a man is a homosexual or not (according to the definition already given), the question arises how the *practising homosexual* may be distinguished from a heterosexual who engages in overt homosexual practices. Careful enquiry should be made as to the nature, frequency and circumstances of his homosexual practices as well as his attitude to both sexes. His erotic attraction towards his own sex is a 'conditio sine qua non' of his anomaly, whether or not he is conscious of such a partiality. The homosexual is relatively rarely

[4] *Ibid.*, p. 12.

found who is so completely attracted towards his own sex as to possess no heterosexual element in his psychosexual make-up. Such an extreme type of homosexual could be defined as

> "one who is entirely unsusceptible to the sexual and emotional attraction of the opposite sex, but is susceptible to the sexual and emotional attraction of his own sex".[5]

Many authors, such as 'Anomaly', conceive this as the common type of homosexual, and are consequently less optimistic as regards a cure to the extent of a heterosexual adjustment in married life. Great harm has been done by conceiving every homosexual as belonging to this *uncommon* category, and thus the fatalism of homosexuality has been falsely asserted for all those who are attracted physically to their own sex, irrespective of their sexual approach to women. In the definition of the homosexual already given, stress is laid on the fact that his major sexual drive is towards his own sex. This does not exclude all heterosexual attraction because, as already stated, homosexuality is not an 'all or none' condition.

Dr. Le Moal's work is also too restrictive as he follows Dalbiez, who requires three characteristics for this extreme type of homosexual: Erotic attraction towards the same sex, complete absence of attraction towards the opposite·sex, and positive disgust for the other sex. He admits, however, that

> "the complete absence of attraction towards the other sex is rare. When it does strongly exist, it is an aversion comparable at all points with that instinctive horror which homosexuality awakens in the normal person. This dis-

[5] *The Invert*, p. 6.

gust does not exclude the possibility of appreciating the other sex aesthetically: but its sculpture, which is justly prized on the artistic plane, becomes repugnant as soon as it is envisaged as an erotic stimulant ".[6]

The third characteristic, which is probably attributable to later environmental influences, is even more infrequent as,

"very often, only erotic attraction for the same sex and the absence of erotic attraction for the other sex are found in the homosexual ".[7]

The advice given to such a homosexual differs from that suggested for the general type of homosexual. He may find the other sex attractive, and in fact often does, but

"it is a common fallacy to believe that if they are introduced to sufficiently seductive members of the opposite sex, this will arouse them. Nothing is further from the truth. They are as unaffected by the charms of a bevy of chorus girls as the normal man would be by a platoon of guardsmen ".[8]

He may desire marriage and a family, yet feel inadequate to the demands involved.

Homosexual activity, though not included in the definition of homosexuality, is often implied. It is not, therefore, true to state that homosexuality is a form of homosexual activity, but truer to call it a sexual state which if committed to act would result in homosexual practices.

[6] 'The Psychiatrist and the Homosexual'. *New Problems in Medical Ethics*, Dom Peter Flood (Cork, 1955) p. 71.
[7] *Ibid.*, p. 72.
[8] *They Stand Apart*. His Honour Judge Tudor Rees and Harley V. Usill. (London, 1955) p. 129.

" Not all homosexuals participate in homosexual practices. Homosexual attraction is a feeling between members of the same sex. Such a feeling expressed by an individual may or may not be reciprocated by the person to whom he . . . is attracted, and the feeling may or may not progress to homosexual activity."[9]

Furthermore, the chaste homosexual does not wish to commit homosexual acts.

This book essentially concerns itself with all those whose major sexual drive is homosexual. It will deal indirectly, however, with all those who engage in homosexual activity, irrespective of where their sexual propensity lies. To devote the book to a consideration of homosexual activity alone would exclude the chaste and continent homosexual and include the heterosexual who commits homosexual acts. Nevertheless, homosexual activity must be included in the study of the homosexual condition because, as will be shown later, a heterosexual can so condition himself by repeated homosexual practices that his major sexual drive becomes homosexual in character.

Besides the practising homosexual, it is found that heterosexuals also engage in homosexual activity. These may be divided into two main classes—the occasional and the habitual.

The *occasional* is one who,

" from motives of curiosity, or in exceptional circumstances —life in the services, or in prison, or in a situation of peculiar temptation or emotion—may engage in one or more homosexual acts, but who easily and rapidly assumes again a

[9] *Homosexuality and Prostitution.* British Medical Association (London, 1955) p. 11.

heterosexual orientation when conditions are normal, and thereafter continues to live a normal heterosexual life ".[10]

These homosexual acts constitute a means of relieving the sexual tension in 'abnormal' conditions and are a very poor second best for his one and only love—woman.[11]
The *habitual* is one who

"may engage regularly in homosexual practices either as a 'tout' or prostitute for money, or for the purpose of blackmail, or in search of new sensual satisfactions, or because simply 'to do evil for evil's sake' has a fascination of its own ".[12]

Their homosexual practices are not instead of, but in addition to, their normal heterosexual practices. Their perverse acts are the inevitable result of a depraved, immoral life and threaten the foundations of human society. Although homosexuals are found in these groups of wicked men, yet it would be wrong to conclude therefore that all homosexuals are lustful, indulgent, sex-crazed monsters whose only aim in life is to warp others with their evil ways. This would prejudice sympathy for the chaste homosexual.

There seems to be another type of person who is neither homosexual nor heterosexual, called the bisexual, whose nature, cause and even existence is very much disputed:

[10] *Sexual Offenders and Social Punishment*, p. 104. (This definition is an extract taken from the Interim Report on 'The Problem of Homosexuality' which was issued by the Church of England Moral Council before the Wolfenden Report was published).
[11] "It is well known that there is usually a certain amount of homosexual activity aboard a ship during long voyages into foreign waters, but the heterosexual activities of sailors when they return to port are even better known." *Society and the Homosexual*, p. 55.
[12] *Sexual Offenders and Social Punishment*, p. 104.

nevertheless, case histories postulate that there are such people. A *bisexual* is:

> "one in whom there appears to be a sexual propensity indiscriminately directed towards the same and the opposite sex ".[13]

His sexual practices as such follow no obvious pattern so that at some period he may carry out *both* homosexual and heterosexual acts, while at other periods, for varying length of time, he may practice one exclusively, the main determinants being the changing circumstances, influences and opportunity. The essential difference between homosexuals and bisexuals is the constancy and direction of their sex drive, which is to the male *alone* in the case of the homosexual, while the bisexual is susceptible to the sex appeal of both sexes. He

> "only manages to steer an irregular course which takes (him) at one time into homosexual currents and at other times into heterosexual ".[14]

Unlike the heterosexual who commits homosexual acts, he is 'attracted sexually' to his own sex, but his condition is generally held to be due to an excessive indulgence in lust since he seeks sex pleasure in all its diverse forms. However, he seems to be less guilty for his homosexual acts than the heterosexual who has no attraction at all for the male and whose homosexual practices are 'sheer' perversity.

Like many normal men, the bisexual cannot bring himself to believe that there are people who are attracted solely to men. Sometimes a weak character, he may marry

[13] *Ibid.*, 103.     [14] *The Invert*, p. 189.

and have children but still retain the capacity for both homosexual and heterosexual practices, so does not deserve the sympathy that would be extended to the homosexual whose sexual attraction is directed exclusively to those of his own sex.

"The bisexual admits his ability to love women: the invert regrets his inability to do so. The bisexual may pride himself on his ability to love males, while the invert sometimes deplores his susceptibility. . . . The bisexual has a choice—the invert has no possible choice at all."[15]

A bisexual may remain ignorant of the appeal of the male sex if his heterosexual life is very dominantly part of him. Some bisexuals, too, even though they possess a very 'weak homosexual' disposition, are found to adopt homosexual practices as prostitutes or blackmailers solely for monetary gain. Their heterosexual re-orientation is made far more difficult by their homosexual indulgences and poor social background.

As we stated before, it is impossible to tell from homosexual practices *alone* whether or not we are dealing with a homosexual, and this must be borne in mind when the prevalence of homosexual practices and the numbers of homosexuals are being discussed. It is an unfortunate phenomenon that many of those who commit overt homosexual acts are basically heterosexual in their sexual drive. Their acts are a deviation from their sexual orientation. As will be shown later, all homosexual acts resulting in orgasm are intrinsically evil and deviations from the

[15] *Ibid.*, p. 57. 'Anomaly' thinks that bisexual acts are no proof of the existence of bisexuality, and that bisexuality neither precedes nor follows homosexuality. When mention is made of bisexuality what one really seems to mean is that the person's behaviour is ambivalent.

natural order of morality, which is essentially heterosexual. If we can prove the existence of a man whose
basic sexual condition is homosexual, then such a person
would *in himself* be a deviation from the natural heterosexuality of men and would be abnormal.

But do such people really exist, and if so, is their condition morally reprehensible, or is homosexuality of such
a nature as to be beyond the conscious control of the
person so afflicted? That is the point to be established.
To make this moral judgement is impossible without a
critical examination of the causality of such a condition,
and immediately we are presented with myriads of
theories all claiming absolute proof by their proponents.
In order to facilitate the moral estimation of the homosexual condition and also to determine the manner of a
possible cure, homosexuals may be divided into two
groups, namely essential and acquired. Some would prefer
to call them respectively 'true' and 'false' homosexuals,
but the latter term is misleading, as acquired homosexuality would seem also a true form of it, in so far as the
acquired homosexual may not be responsible for his
condition.

*Essential homosexuals* would be those whose condition
is either genetically determined, or whose homosexuality
is caused by early environmental factors and influences
outside the scope of conscious memory. In neither case,
nor in a combination and interaction of both, would the
subject be morally guilty of the origin of his homosexual
condition. Since it is generally agreed that homosexuality
is not an 'all or none' condition, the British Medical
Association rightly stresses the danger of a bad early
environment which would adversely affect the child with

homosexual tendencies and result in a homosexual condition.

> "If early environment influences, outside the scope of conscious memory," it says, "are brought to bear on a tendency to homosexuality, they may have harmful effects. For example, in some young children the development of their personality is disturbed by exaggerated emotional attachment to one parent, by the absence of one parent or some other abnormal factors in their environment."[16]

*Acquired homosexuals* would be those in whom the tendency to commit homosexual acts is predominantly determined by new factors arising in later life, that is, later childhood, adolescence, or manhood. One cannot completely exclude certain medical or early environmental factors from this group as contributing causes, but the main determining factors which influence the person to commit overt sexual acts are of a later environmental nature.

On examination of case histories, there are times when it is extremely difficult to distinguish the ' essential ' from the ' acquired ', so that

> "a man who in middle life commits a homosexual offence for the first time may at first sight seem to belong to the acquired group, but investigation may show that he is actually an essential homosexual, and that mental or other stress has only now weakened his resistance and self-discipline".[17]

One of the big weaknesses of the British Medical Association Commission, however, was an undue readiness to call

---

[16] *Homosexuality and Prostitution*, p. 12.
[17] *Ibid.*, p. 12.

certain cases 'essential' when there seemed no foundation for such a diagnosis.

Some doctors—very much a minority—exaggeratedly stress the innate character of homosexuality, and reject any influence from environmental factors. Such a restriction would not help the main object of this book, which is an attempt to assess the moral responsibility of the homosexual for his condition. Early environmental factors outside the scope of conscious memory are therefore linked with genetical elements. This does not prejudice the causal influence of physical factors since it prescinds from the fact whether genetical or environmental causes alone or together cause the homosexual condition. As will be shown in later chapters, the case for biochemical-biological causality is unproven and extremely doubtful for the common type of homosexuality.

CHAPTER TWO

# The Extent of the Homosexual
# Problem in England

~~~~~~~~~~~~~~~~~~~~~~~~~~~~~~~~~~~~~~~~~~~~~~~~~~~~~~~~~~

To attempt to assess the sexual inclinations of a total
population is difficult, if not impractical. It becomes a
mammoth task where homosexuality is concerned. Homosexual acts are by nature more secretive partly because of
the social condemnation attached to those who participate
in such practices. It is practically impossible to arrive at
any reasonably accurate estimate of the extent either of
the homosexual condition or of the frequency of homosexual acts committed in England. There is disagree-
ment as to the number and validity of inferences that
can be drawn from the available statistics. Carefully used
social statistics, however, may be helpful in forming an
unbiassed judgement on a controversial subject provided they are scientifically sound, and not pushed beyond
their limits in the resulting conclusions.

There has been no enquiry into the sex life of the
British Male on the scale undertaken by Kinsey in
America, and his findings have been extensively criticized
as unreliable. If a definite answer were to be given as to
the number of homosexuals and their practices, and if it
were to be decided whether or not there has been a real
increase in the homosexual problem since the war, then

the statistics would have to be more accurate and comprehensive, enquiring into the nature, circumstances and attitude of those who engage in overt homosexual acts. Only then could it be categorically stated what is the proportion of heterosexuals to homosexuals who commit homosexual acts but remain heterosexual in their main sexual drive.

All are agreed, however, that there is an astronomical disparity between illicit homosexual acts that occur and those that are detected. A cursory examination of the *police statistics* over the past twenty years shows an alarming progressive increase in the number of indictable homosexual offences, and if undetected acts are increasing in the same proportion as the detected acts then the position is most disquietening.[1]

Those homosexuals who influence medical or pastoral opinion, or come into conflict with the law, form a small part of the homosexual world. Criminal statistics, if quoted and considered by themselves alone, are thus of little scientific value, not only because they deal with a minority and any induction may be invalid, but also because they ignore the sexual bias of the criminal offender. Moreover, it is an unrepresentative minority insofar as it consists mainly of the more blatant and unrestrained cases, and especially of the corrupters of young boys, who do not seem typical of homosexuals as a whole. In the opinion of 'Anomaly' the pseudo-homosexual and the bisexual form the largest part of those indicted of homosexual practices.[2] Yet there is no doubt that the

---

[1] " The number of detected homosexual acts must be only a fraction of the total number of such acts committed in public and in private." *Ibid.*, p. 22.

[2] *The Invert*, p. 16.

problem exists, and the only argument is about its extent.

The homosexuals who steep themselves in sentimental literature on the subject, and belong to one of the levels of the homosexual underworld, are notorious for exaggerating their numbers through wishful thinking.  They attempt to paint everyone of note, past and present, with the same brush.  The champions of their cause in demanding a new moral code claim that society cannot afford to ignore, or even worse punish, such a vast army of homosexuals.  At the other extreme we find many normal men who sincerely hold that they have never met a homosexual.

It is tempting to construct hypotheses on the basis of the police statistics, and while the surfeit of speculation in the literature on homosexuality in recent times merits disapproval, yet we shall attempt to do so while realizing the dangers involved.  As already stated, only a minority of the homosexual world falls into police hands, and this limits the inference that may legitimately be drawn. Only a limited number of prisoners are medically or psychologically examined and even then—

"There can be no guarantee that the individuals selected for study have told the whole truth or that when they have tried to do so their introspection has been accurate or complete.  Moreover the capacity for self-expression varies considerably as between one individual and another: dull and inarticulate persons are often unable to give more than the crudest account of their psychosexual reactions, and an accurate assessment of propensities or of the significance of behaviour is correspondingly difficult.  Quantitative estimates based on subjective evidence of this sort are therefore in themselves liable to a considerable degree of error: and when applied to the population as a whole the final result may be dangerously misleading."[3]

It is impossible to determine, therefore, with any certainty from police statistics alone what proportion of the total population of the country may be said to be homosexual in their sexual propensity.

Police figures for heterosexual offences in 1953 (10,135) are four times greater than in the years from 1930 to 1934. Homosexual offences for the same period increased seven-fold—from 748 to 5,680—nearly double the rate of increase in heterosexual indictable acts. These figures are more disturbing when it is remembered that illegal sexual offences are more difficult to trace where consenting parties are concerned, and there have in fact been very few prosecutions of consenting adults in private.[4]   This is confirmed by Dr. Radzinowicz who investigated a broad sample of sexual offences known to the police in 1947. 3,000 cases involving over 2,000 persons were examined in fourteen major police areas in England, and only two such cases were found in the sample taken, thus showing the rarity of prosecutions of consenting homosexual adults in private.[5]   Neither the figures for the heterosexual or homosexual, however, afford the basis for a correct estimate of the total incidence of such sexual offences.

The efficiency of the police methods of detection and

---

[3] *Wolfenden Report*, p. 18.

[4] "Covert Homosexuality . . . is rarely prosecuted and I have not experienced a single case in which two adult men were charged with committing homosexual acts behind closed doors."—F. H. Taylor, Medical Officer, H.M. Prison, Brixton.  'Homosexual Offences and their relation to Psychotherapy.' *British Med. Journal.*  Vol. 2, 1947 (p. 509).

[5] *Sexual Offences.*  Cambridge Dept. of Criminal Science.  Edited by Dr. L. Radzinowicz.  (Macmillan, 1957).

the intensity of police activity will obviously increase the number of detected offences.

> "It was to be expected that the more intensive training given to police officers in recent years, particularly in methods of detection, would result in the discovery of a higher proportion of offences: but this does not necessarily indicate that more offences have occurred".[6]

The extent to which the police follow up suspicions of homosexual behaviour varies considerably, depending especially upon the outlook of the senior officers.

> "Sometimes even within a given police force the intensity of action varies from time to time along with the ups and downs of public indignation aroused, or public annoyance caused, by the behaviour of the offenders."[7]

Under such circumstances it would be wrong to argue from police statistics alone that there was an overall increase in homosexual behaviour since before the war, or that it was most prevalent in the areas where the highest number of cases are recorded by the police. Yet the Wolfenden Report states what is most likely to give a correct picture of the true state of affairs, namely that:

> "Most of us think it improbable that the increase in the number of offences recorded as known to the police can be explained entirely by greater police activity, though we all think it very unlikely that homosexual behaviour has increased proportionately to the dramatic rise in the number of offences recorded as known to the police."[8]

[6] *Wolfenden Report*, p. 19.
[7] *Ibid.*, p. 19.
[8] *Ibid.*, p. 20.

D

By assessing police statistics correctly and attributing to them their due importance we are able to draw some valid conclusions. Set against the background of a general loosening of moral standards we feel justified in holding that they indicate a real increase in homosexual practices in recent years.

Apart from the criminal statistics, we have also at our disposal social surveys, such as those of Hirschfeld in Germany and Kinsey in America, which may help us in the estimation of the number of homosexuals and the prevalence of homosexual practices in England.

One of the first estimates of homosexuals was undertaken by Dr. Hirschfeld who compiled a questionnaire of 130 questions which was answered by 10,000 men and women in Germany, and from which he concluded that out of a population of nearly sixty million, there were nearly a million and a half completely or largely homosexual, that is about *1.5 per cent of the population*. He also made a large number of separate estimates among different classes of people and found that the proportion of homosexuals and bisexuals to the total population ranged from one to five per cent.[9]   The police in Berlin at that time tolerated homosexual prostitution on the same basis as female prostitution, and Hirschfeld estimated the number as twenty thousand while more recently Wener Picton says that it is in the region of six thousand.[10]

The late Havelock Ellis estimated that of the population of England, the numbers of homosexuals showed a proportion of from two to four per cent, while in about

[9] *Psychology of Sex*. Havelock Ellis, (A Mentor book. New American Library. Third Printing 1956), p. 162.
[10] *Ibid.*, p. 163.

fifty per cent of those cases homosexual practices did not occur.   Dr. Neustatter remarks that the wide divergencies which the various figures show, even at the outset, "indicate some of the complexity of the whole problem and what variations of opinion and interpretation of the observed phenomena exist".[11]

The report, however, to attract the most attention and comment is that submitted by Kinsey, Pomeroy and Martin, which is embodied in their book *Sexual Behaviour in the Human Male*, published in 1948, and which arranges its subjects according to case histories in seven grades, ranging from the exclusively heterosexual to the exclusive homosexual with five intermediate types.

1. 37 per cent had some homosexual experience resulting in orgasm after the advent of adolescence while in addition another 13 per cent were erotically attracted to males without any such sexual acts, so that fifty per cent were affected by homosexuality whether under the aspect of practice or attraction.

2. 25 per cent had *more than incidental* homosexual practices or attractions *for at least three years between the ages of 16 and 55*.   This period of three years is understood for the next four grades.

3. 18 per cent are *as much homosexual* as heterosexual in their case histories.

4. 13 per cent *more homosexual* than heterosexual.

5. 10 per cent are *more or less exclusively* homosexual.

6. 8 per cent are *exclusively* homosexual.

7. 4 per cent are exclusively homosexual throughout their lives, and not like the other groups which only cover a period of at least three years.   Kinsey held that "6·3

[11] *They Stand Apart*, pp. 69-70.

per cent of the total number of orgasms are derived from homosexual reactions",[12] and of those unmarried by the age of thirty-five he found over half had had some homosexual experience, while only ten per cent of married men between 21-25 committed homosexual acts. Among single men Kinsey found that incidence increased with age, so that while 27·5 per cent of single men between the ages of 21-25 indulge in homosexual experiences, this percentage is increased to 38·7 per cent between the ages of 36-40. Widowers or those who were divorced between the ages of 26-30 had a percentage of 17·6, while it was reduced to 6·2 per cent in the 36-40 age group.[13]

In a recent enquiry in Sweden it was discovered that 4 per cent of all men had both homosexual and heterosexual impulses, while 1 per cent was exclusively homosexual. Later, however, official sources in Sweden said that other information available seemed to indicate that these figures were too low.

Taking these figures as a yardstick, if one in every twenty-five in England and Wales were exclusively homosexual, then this would mean that there are over 650,000 homosexuals in these countries, but the British Medical Association observes that if a study similar to Kinsey's were made in England, the figures would be found to be much lower:

"though even if the United States figures were reduced by 50 per cent, the number of persons involved would be sufficiently high to represent a serious social problem".[14]

[12] *Psychiatry & Catholicism.* Odenwald and Vanderveldt, (New York, 1952), p. 381.
[13] *Society and the Homosexual*, p. 29.
[14] *Homosexuality and Prostitution*, p. 20.

F. H. Taylor, reporting on Brixton Prison for the year 1946, said that out of a total number of 5,023 remand and trial prisoners received during the year, 96 were charged with homosexual offences, which is less than two per cent of the total.[15]   This, however, may not be of great significance, as some prisons are more favoured than others by the authorities for the incarceration and treatment of these offenders.

The Wolfenden Report commenting on the Kinsey work says:

"Dr. Kinsey's figures have aroused opposition and scepticism.  But it was noteworthy that some of our medical witnesses expressed the view that something very like these figures would be established in this country if similar enquiries were made.  The majority while stating quite frankly that they did not really know, indicated that their impression was that his figures would be on the high side for Great Britain."[16]

*Kinsey's statistics* are constantly recurring in the various studies in England devoted to the homosexual problem, and many books that advocate a new moral code for the homosexual are based on his findings.  It is important, therefore, to determine the value which should be attributed to his work, and to decide whether or not his approach is of such a scientific nature that it will help efforts to arrive at some estimation of homosexual preva-

---

[15] 'Homosexual Offences and their relation to Psychotherapy'—*British Medical Journal* (1947) Vol. 2, p. 525.  'Anomaly' is very loath to make a decision as to the number of homosexuals, yet is quite convinced that many estimates are grossly exaggerated because no distinction has been drawn between homosexuals and bisexuals; but he suggests, with diffidence, that "the percentage of inverts in the male population is not more than five ".  *The Invert*, p. 14.

[16] *Op. cit.*, p. 17.

lence—whether of condition or practice. Even if his statistics were correct—and they are very much challenged —he makes no reference to the motivation, nature or circumstances of the homosexual acts recorded by him. His survey merely serves to highlight a vast amount of unnatural sexual acts. He ignores the personal element in the sexual act, and repudiates human psychology by considering man no better than an animal. He argues that homosexual acts are 'natural' because they are commonly practised by men and animals.

Kinsey concludes from what men actually do to what men are, and claims that the standards of human behaviour should be adapted to social behaviour as it exists, so that if the majority—at least a great proportion—of men commit homosexual acts, then such acts are not immoral. In other words unnatural homosexual practices would become moral and natural because they were prevalent. Since the chief criterion of sexuality is apparently an orgasm, then sex is something to be let out and the more the better. The vast propaganda which preceded Kinsey's work clearly showed that his approach was of the 'best-seller' category rather than scientific. Certain flaws were pointed out to him after the publication of his first volume, but the second volume showed no improvement in scientific approach.[17] In brief, Kinsey's work is of little use to a scientific study of the homosexual problem.

One would expect that another possible source of information as to the extent of homosexuality would be furnished by medical and psychiatric evidence. The

[17] "He appears to have heeded scarcely a word of the scholarly analyses and wise counsel of such penetrating critics as Dr. Robert P. Knight, Dr. Lawrence Kubie, Lionel Trilling and numerous others." *Medical Ethics*, Edwin F. Healy, S. J., (Chicago, 1956), p. 294.

British Medical Association states in the introduction to its Report—*Homosexuality and Prostitution*—that as regards the position of the medical profession "homosexuality is an essentially social rather than medical problem".[18] The value of medical and psychiatric theories with reference to prevalence, causality and cure is strictly limited by the following observations of the Wolfenden Report:

> "first, that in general practice male homosexuals form a very small fraction of the doctor's patients: secondly, that in psychiatric practice male homosexuality is a primary problem in a very small proportion of the cases seen: and thirdly, that only a very small percentage of homosexuals consult doctors about their condition".[19]

The following statement of the British Medical Association clearly demonstrates their acknowledged incapacity to deal with the problem.

> "The attempt to suppress homosexuality by law can only be one factor in diminishing this problem. A public opinion against homosexual practices is a greater safeguard, and this can be achieved by promoting the minds, motives and wills of the people with a desire for clean and unselfish living. At the present time doctors observe their patients in an environment favourable to sexual indulgence and surrounded by irresponsibility, selfishness and a pre-occupation with immediate materialistic satisfaction. There is

[18] *Homosexuality and Prostitution*, p. 8.
"No doubt we on Medical Boards saw but a fraction of the homosexuals in the army, but the fraction represented a number sufficiently high to astonish and distress me, who in twenty-five years of private practice had found this form of pathological sexuality extraordinarily rare. . . . To me it constitutes a phenomenon of such importance that no patriotic body interested in the mental and physical hygiene of the people can afford to disregard it." *In My Fashion.* Herbert M. Moran, (London, 1946), p. 124.
[19] *Op. cit.*, p. 20.

also no lack of stimulation to sexual appetite. Suggestive advertisements abound on the street hoardings and in the Underground; provocative articles and illustrations appear in the daily and especially the Sunday newspapers; magazines and cheap novels with lurid covers frequently provide suggestive reading matter; and the erotic nature of many films and stage shows is but thinly veiled. This background tends to increase heterosexual over-activity, while for homosexuals it fans the fire of resentment at the latitude allowed to heterosexual indulgence when their own sexual activities are condemned and they are regarded as criminals. . . . People who are mainly concerned with themselves and their sensations associate together and obtain from each other the physical and emotional experience they desire. Personal discipline and unselfishness have little place in their thoughts. If this behaviour is multiplied on a national scale, the problem to society is apparent for widespread irresponsibility and selfishness can only demoralize and weaken the nation. What is needed is responsible citizenship where concern for the nation's welfare and the needs of others takes priority over selfish interests and self-indulgence."[20]

The individual's right to happiness must not blind a man to his social duties and responsibilities. If it does, then it is not surprising that society has little time for these men.

Many who are firmly convinced that homosexual practices are on the increase find supporting evidence for their assumption *if homosexuality be considered primarily a moral problem*. Police statistics have been examined but the most perfect legal system deals only with failures and breakdowns, whereas the root of the homosexual trouble is traceable to the fact that behind the majority of indictable homosexual offences there lie unsatisfactory and

[20] *Homosexuality and Prostitution*, p. 10.

broken homes. One of the greatest contributory factors to man's inability to make a satisfactory heterosexual adjustment is an unhappy home life; divorced parents;[21] where the child has been deprived of his father's influence due to prolonged war service; where parents are away for long periods at work and feel unable to cope with ordinary family problems. It is only too true that society gets the homosexual it deserves. The extent of divorce in England is shown by the fact that the ratio of new marriages to divorces in 1871 was 1150:1, while in 1952 it had become 10:1, so that nowadays 20,000 children are affected annually.[22]

This century has seen two world wars which left their marks both on the families and on the soldiers who, perhaps for the first time in an all-male environment, engaged in homosexual practices. In some cases, these homosexual practices carried over into peace-time because the subjects were unwilling or unable to make a satisfactory heterosexual adjustment.[23]

In the general loosening of moral standards, it inevitably follows that men are less discreet about their sexual practices. In a healthy moral atmosphere which would condemn rather than condone sexual promiscuity, there is less likelihood that such tendencies would so easily

[21] The Report of the Research Council into Marriage and Human Relations (The Chessar Report) categorically states that separation or divorce is more destructive of a child's happiness than the death of either parent.

[22] 1857-1957: A Century of Family Law. Edited by R. H. Graveson and F. R. Crane, (London, 1957).

[23] " To the extent that a person of either sex has engaged in sex variant activity, he or she is less likely to make a satisfactory heterosexual adjustment. The chances of making such an adjustment are less to the extent that substitute sexual behaviour has been prolonged." Sex Variants. George W. Henry. (New York 1948), p. 1027.

crystallize into activity.  Partly for this reason we know
remarkably little about the incidence of homosexuality
in the last century.  The attitude of society today seems
more tolerant towards sexual irregularities in general, and
there would hardly have been such a concerted appeal
for a change in the law of England if there were little
chance of success.  If acquired homosexuality is accepted
—that is to say if a man can become a conditioned homosexual by repeated acts—then the laxer the moral order
the greater the number of conditioned homosexuals.[24]
Books and magazines that glorify homosexual 'love' have
a wider reading public, and the stage witnesses the 'drag
act' in which men dress as women with the obvious
implications unconcealed.

The Wolfenden Report states that those

"who have the impression of a growth in homosexual practices find it supported by at least three wider considerations.
First, in the general loosening of former moral standards,
it would not be surprising to find that leniency towards
sexual irregularities in general included also an increased
tolerance of homosexual behaviour and that greater tolerance
had increased the practice.  Secondly, the conditions of war
time, with broken families and prolonged separation of the
sexes, may well have occasioned homosexual behaviour
which in some cases has been carried over into peace time.
Thirdly, it is likely that the emotional insecurity, community instability and weakening of the family, inherent
in the social changes of our civilization, have been factors
contributing to an increase in homosexual behaviour."[25]

[24] "There is evidence that pre-marital chastity has decreased rapidly in
the last fifty years."  'Pre-Marital chastity', *The Practitioner*, No. 1030;
Vol. 172.  April, 1954, p. 419.  Alfred Torrie, M.B., D.P.M., Physical-
Superintendent, The Retreat, York.
[25] *Op. cit.*, p. 20.

What can be said in conclusion with some degree of certainty as regards the prevalence of homosexuality in Great Britain? The numbers of homosexuals and the incidence of homosexual behaviour is of such proportions as to present a serious moral and social problem. Homosexuality is more freely discussed today than formerly, but this of itself is not a criterion of any real increase unless it is, as we believe, the outcome of a laxer moral attitude to immoral sexual practices. It seems indubitably true that homosexual practices are more frequent than formerly: that there has been a consequent rise in the number of those conditioned by such behaviour yet not to the extent suggested by the police statistics.[26] The homosexual is still relatively scarce and forms a very small but vociferous section of human society. Homosexual behaviour, which is engaged in by a wider group than those whose major sexual drive is towards their own sex, is still only

"practised by a small proportion of the population, and should be seen in proper perspective; neither ignored nor given a disproportionate amount of public attention".[27]

[26] 'Anomaly' is of the opinion "that the incidence of primal sex confusion is no greater than it used to be, but is more in evidence because of the prevailing flux in sexual morality. Estimates of the incidence of inversion will vary according to the significance given to homosexual actions. My opinion is that such actions are not confined to inverts and that many inverts do not practise them". *The Invert*, p. 215.

'Anomaly' holds innate homosexuality alone and therefore denies the conditioning influence of homosexual practices. For him greater incidence of homosexual activity does not result in a greater number of homosexuals.

[27] *Wolfenden Report*, p. 20.

CHAPTER THREE

# Genetic Causality—The Chromosomal Theory

THE causality of homosexuality introduces a problem which is both complex and controversial, yet the urgency of attempting a solution is of primary importance. The moral judgement of the homosexual condition as regards personal responsibility will depend on the etiological factors involved, and will also determine the nature of the therapy to be applied to the homosexual. Many authors stress that there is no such person as a homosexual as such, since each individual is so different in his abnormality as to constitute a 'law unto himself'. While it is true that each homosexual has his own peculiar family background, personal history and physical constitution, all of which may, in fact, have contributed in different and varying degrees to his homosexual propensity, yet this is no reason why a prognosis should not be attempted.

Homosexuality is a sexual aberration, and is no different, as we shall see, from other sexual abnormalities. To set homosexuality apart from other sexual problems is to presume that it is different, a presumption without proof. In sexual abnormalities certain recurring symptoms can be observed in the tangled skein of possible causes, which

34

makes it lawful to conclude that they conduce or cause
a man to develop his existing sexual tendencies. Homosexuality is considered by us in terms of the person
concerned; as in other moral problems, the human
element is never forgotten, yet a moral judgement is given.
This fundamental notion involves the whole morality of
human acts; any act to be moral or immoral in a formal
sense must involve free will. If any aspect of human
behaviour is to be excluded from such a judgement, then
positive reasons must be given for such an exclusion,
since the objective violation of the moral code involves presumed subjective guilt until the contrary is
proved.

The opposing views as to the origin of the homosexual
condition are divided into psychogenic and organogenic,
according as their proponents consider the sexual propensity to arise from environmental or inborn organic factors.
One of the main aims of this book is to establish a moral
judgement on the individual's responsibility for his homosexual condition. Consequent on the distinction made in
the previous chapter (p. 17) between essential and acquired
homosexuality, early environmental factors are not
divorced from the constitutional elements that may be
involved. To consider the physical and psychological
factors separately is not to deny their interaction and
mutual dependence.

On the contrary, it will be shown that whereas heredity
determines what one can do, yet environment determines
to a large extent what in fact one does. Most authoritative sources today admit that not only are there a number
of different factors which tend to create a homosexual
pattern, but that homosexual practices are nearly always

the result of two or more of these factors. Even if it is established, for example, that the organogenic case alone is unproven for the common types of homosexuality, yet the whole medical edifice is not thereby destroyed. While it may not be everything, it may contribute something to explain why people are attracted sexually towards their own sex. Some inborn constitutional factors may be present, as in other cases in medicine, to explain for example, why one individual gets tuberculosis, while another equally exposed does not. It must also be remembered that

"throughout psychiatry one finds that the structure of the personality is an interplay between environment and constitutional endowment; so much so that it is almost possible to devise an equation that constitution multiplied by environment = a constant".[1]

Very few present day authorities do, in fact, claim that all homosexuality is solely genetically determined, or that environment is the only causative element involved. Of the extremists, it may be suggested that the judgements put forward reflect the personal prejudiced views of their holders rather than a true assessment of the facts, often warped to fit a previously-held theory.

Most advocates of the constitutional or genetic explanation of homosexuality, rebelling against the exclusive claims of a purely environmental causality, claim that there are some homosexuals, whose numbers and

[1] 'Homosexuality: Incidence and Causation. Hereditary and Constitutional Factors.' W. Lindesay Neustatter, M.D., Physician in Psychological Medicine, Royal Northern Hospital, and Queen Mary's Hospital for the East End, London; Consultant Psychiatrist, St. Ebba's Hospital, Epsom. *They Stand Apart*, p. 78.

degrees vary with different authors, who are so biologically determined as to form an intersex variety of the
human race. These homosexuals would belong to what
Hirschfeld called the 'Third Sex'. They claim, therefore, that the existence of inborn, organically constituted
homosexuals must be admitted, in addition to the homosexual whose main determining factor has been environment. If this is true, then the therapy that can be applied
is not confined to the psychiatrist or psychoanalyst.
Some, however, like Hirschfeld and other advocates of
therapeutic nihilism, held that such a homosexual was so
constitutionally determined that nothing in the way of a
cure could be achieved.

> "All these authors have to offer to homosexuals is the
> advice to indulge in their tendencies, but in such a safe
> way as to stay out of the hands of the law, and avoid social
> ostracism."[2]

Other writers are not so pessimistic, and the present-day
tendency is towards a more optimistic view of achieving
results. Dr. Curran and Dr. Whitby in their note appen-
ded to the Wolfenden Report claim that

> "the outlook for the adolescent and transitional homosexual
> is often very good. . . . Complete pessimism in all regards
> is only justified in some homosexuals".[3]

Before considering in detail the various evidences of
modern physicians and endocrinologists, a short summary
of the development of the organogenic position may prove
helpful. Acquired homosexuality seems to have been the

---

[2] 'Homosexuality: Therapy'. *Psychiatry and Catholicism*, p. 388.
[3] Op. cit., p. 76.

only type acknowledged until the influence of Krafft-Ebing's work *Psycopathia Sexualis* began to be felt. Until then, the homosexual received little sympathy or consideration, as his condition was considered to be the result either of masturbation or sexual excesses which produced impotence in normal coition. Krafft-Ebing at first considered homosexual practices to be necessarily connected with neuropathic or psychopathic states, but concluded from a large number of clinical cases that as well as the acquired type, there were also inborn organic homosexuals. Thereafter in this century the tendency has been to minimize the former category, and to stress the importance and predominance of the congenital homosexual. This tendency is very marked in Moll's treatise.

In 1914 Hirschfeld compiled a book, *Der Homosexualitat*, in which he deduced from a personal study and knowledge of homosexuals that there was always a congenital element present in homosexuality, and this point of view was shared by Maranon. Others, like Block and Näcks, who began with the theory that homosexuality was exclusively or at least chiefly an acquired condition, became later upholders of the genetic basis of causality, to such an extent that Bloch considered anyone who engaged in homosexual practices as a pseudo-homosexual if the congenital element were missing. Näcks also

"considered that we have to distinguish not between congenital and acquired inversion, but between true and false, and . . . regarded homosexuality appearing late in life as not acquired, but 'retarded' or delayed homosexuality on a congenital basis ".[4]

[4] The short history is taken from Havelock Ellis's book *Psychology of Sex*, pp. 164-5.

The upholders of *the chromosomal theory* explain the causality of homosexuality by considering the male homosexual to be a sex intergrade. It finds many supporters in medical circles, and Hirschfeld was its great champion. Biologically speaking, a male homosexual is really a woman in disguise, whose genetic sex does not agree with his physical body-build. In every sex chromosome, whether XX or XY, there is held to be the physical basis of an impulse which tends to impose the male or female type on the developing individual. A male homosexual, therefore, is a 'male gone wrong' in the chromosomal sphere. Normal men have an X chromosome from the mother, and a Y chromosome from the father, thus constituting the normal XY chromosomal pattern. In the same way normal females are of the XX type, receiving an X chromosome from the father as well as the mother. The male homosexual even though he may have well-developed sex organs, and possess no secondary female sexual characteristics, is still chromosomally a woman. He is psychosexually attracted to the male, which for him is the 'opposite sex', due to his chromosomal pattern being XX. This hypothesis is also supported by Havelock Ellis to explain away the difficulty why so many masculine types are found among male homosexuals. He calls a homosexual a somatic male with the psyche of a female. The basis of the whole theory rests, *not on experiments on human beings*, but on gipsy moths carried out by Goldschmidt.

"The degree of intersexuality in the gipsy moth depends on the stage of development at which sex differentiation is disturbed. Should this crucial stage be reached very

E

early in development, the end-result is complete sex-reversal."[5]

In such a case the sex-chromosome should read XX for males and XY for females.

Can the chromosomal theory be proved in the case of individual homosexuals, or of homosexuals as a group? It will remain an unproven hypothesis unless experimentation is carried out on people who are known to be homosexuals, and a causal connection between their homosexual condition and their intersexuality firmly established. This medical examination is quite impossible at the present moment

"since the ability to detect alterations at the gene level lies far beyond our relatively crude method of studying intermitotic nuclei".[6]

Apart from that, if scientific investigation were possible, is homosexuality a suitable subject for study at chromosomal level? Again, the answer is in the negative. The British Medical Association's Report commenting on 'The Case for a Genetic Basic', holds that

"homosexuality is in fact an unsuitable trait for precise genetical study because its character is complex, it does not show clear segregation, and it is much influenced by environment".[7]

Homosexuality is rarely by itself alone a subject for

[5] 'Chromosomal Sex in Transvestites', *Lancet*, Vol. I, p. 1110. May 20th, 1954. Murray L. Barr, Professor of Microscopic Anatomy; Edgar Hobbs, Professor of Psychiatry and Preventative Medicine. Both of University of Western Ontario, London, Canada.

[6] *Ibid.*, p. 1110.

[7] *Homosexuality and Prostitution*, p. 24.

clinical treatment. The homosexual, secretive and disinclined to give information about himself, is generally unwilling to undergo medical treatment unless he is in trouble with the police authorities, or unless his condition is associated with an intercurrent psychopathic condition. The genetical basis of his psychosexual abnormality, therefore, can only be studied by implication in so far as it is a symptom of a more inclusive psychopathic disorder. Even if science allowed *certain* chromosomal knowledge of psychopaths, which it *cannot*, the only proof for the present hypothesis would be restricted to one of mere implication.

Would the chromosomal hypothesis seem to explain the common types of homosexuality? Even where secondary female sexual characteristics are very much in evidence in some homosexuals, and *they form a minority* of the homosexual world,

"there seems to be no reason to believe that the common types of homosexuality have a genetical basis of this kind".[8]

*A fortiori*, all are agreed, this is true of the majority of homosexuals who show no secondary female sexual characteristics whatsoever.

The preceding statements of the British Medical Association's Report on Homosexuality receive added force when it is remembered that this medical source commenting on a purely medical aspect admits that it cannot establish any definite medical scientific proof of the chromosomal theory. Furthermore it holds that present scientific methods are unable to carry out such an examination. One would expect to find innumerable books by

[8] *Ibid.*, p. 26.

psychiatrists and psychoanalysts attacking the intersex theory, yet the British Medical Association itself condemns the chromosomal theory as a possible medical explanation of homosexual propensities.   In general the whole tenor of the Report does attempt to establish some physical constitutional basis, but whatever it may be, it does not claim it at the chromosomal level.

As regards the Chromosomal Theory in general, therefore, it may be said that it must be considered as an unproved and, with the present state of medical knowledge, unprovable hypothesis.   It seems no more than mere speculation and affords no basis for any serious moral principle at its present stage of development.

The British Medical Association's Report enumerates *two specific scientific experiments* which confirm the rejection of the intersex theory.   These experiments demonstrate clearly that, as far as present-day medical science allows the conclusion, there is no causal connection between the sex-chromosome complex and the homosexual propensity.   In other words, scientific evidence, scanty as it may be, is positively against the chromosomal explanation of homosexuality.

The first experiment was carried out by Barr and Hobbs on five cases of 'marked transvestism'.   They applied skin-biopsy tests of chromosomal sex to the male transvestites because of their interest in the

> "theory that the male transvestite may represent an extreme type of intersexuality or sex reversal in which an embryo with the XX sex-chromosome complex is diverted in the male direction at a very early stage of embryonic development".[9]   "Skin-biopsy specimens were studied in five cases

[9] 'Chromosomal Sex in Transvestites', *Lancet*, 1, (1954), p. 1109.

of genuine male transvestism. Sections were stained by the Feulgen method, with haematoxylin and eosin, and were of excellent quality technically. In each case the epidermal nuclei had a typical male morphology, whence it is inferred that these five patients had the male XY sex-chromosome complex. Though it is now reasonably certain that male transvestites have XY sex-chromosomes, this by no means rules out the possibility that the abnormality may have a genetical basis."[10]

While there is no necessary connection between transvestism and homosexuality, nevertheless it is not an uncommon phenomenon for a transvestite to be a homosexual. In fact, the male transvestite, according to most authors, is the most extreme type of homosexual, as he has no desire to be other than he is, and even desires the body of a female. It is quite logical, therefore, for the British Medical Association's Report to conclude from this experiment that:

"similar results might be expected from a comparable study of males selected on account of homosexual psychological orientation, but otherwise normal".[11]

In other words, the homosexual is a chromosomal male. The second experiment was performed by Paul Polani, W. F. Hunter and Bernard Lennox on three patients with Turner's Syndrome.[12]

---

[10] *Ibid.*, p. 1110.

[11] 'The case for a genetic basis', *Homosexuality and Prostitution*, p. 26.

[12] Turner's Syndrome is a condition in which there is agenesis of the female gonads (i.e. ovaries), due to congenital absence or to failure of maturation of rudimentary ovaries. There is an associated dwarfism due to pituitary defect, and various other congenital defects are present, e.g. narrowing of the aorta with defective development, etc.

"It seems theoretically possible that at least some of the patients with Turner's Syndrome are genetic males, who, because their gonads have been damaged or have not developed in early intra-uterine life, have not acquired a masculine genital tract."[13]  The three cases examined were aged 20, 18 and 10, but in the latter case "absolute proof of ovarian agenesis is not at hand because of the patient's age".  Polani took specimens of skin, and having prepared them scientifically for examination, submitted them to Hunter and Lennox who "were unaware of the nature of the investigation, or the sex of the persons involved".[14] They gave the judgement on the chromosomal sex and

"in the three cases studied, the discrepancy found between apparent sex and the results of skin-biopsy suggests that something went wrong in their sexual differentiation".[15]

Here we have the reverse of Barr and Hobb's findings with the transvestite, for while the sex-chromosome of the apparent females is XY, or abnormal, there is no mention of the problem of any sexual abnormality arising.

The importance of these two experiments may be estimated from the fact that, even though they are limited in the number of subjects examined, it must be remembered that very little work in this sphere has been done in

[13] 'Chromosomal Sex in Turner's Syndrome with coarctation of the aorta'. *Lancet*, 2 (1954) pp. 120-21.  Paul E. Polani, Department of Child Health, Guy's Hospital Medical School.  W. F. Hunter & Bernard Lennox, Department of Pathology, Post-graduate Medical School of London.
[14] *Ibid.*, p. 120.
[15] *Ibid.*, p. 121.

the medical field.  They were the only two experiments mentioned in the British Medical Report, so they cannot be considered to be the mere expression of the findings of their authors since by their inclusion in the Report they have merited official approval.  The experiments show that there is no connection between the sex-chromosome complex and homosexuality, because in the first experiment with transvestites where there is a marked homosexual attraction, the male sex-chromosome is XY; in the second experiment, the female sex-chromosome is the male XY with no apparent consequent abnormal sexuality.  'Genetic sex', therefore, does not mean that the sex desire will correspond.  In a word homosexuality does not follow the so-called 'genetic sex'.

It would be false to conclude that the chromosomal theory is *absolutely excluded* on medical grounds, because as we have said little research has been undertaken. Future investigations may contradict our present knowledge.  Yet the only possible conclusion to be drawn is that present scientific knowledge demands another explanation for homosexuality.

Nor do we know enough of *familial incidence* of homosexuality, which is considered more fully at a later stage, to provide any supporting evidence for a chromosomal explanation.  Thomas Lang's experiments in 1940[16] are no more than suggestive that homosexuality may run in families among brothers.  They are certainly not conclusive.  They have not been confirmed by other workers such as Dr. Eliot Slater and Roy A. Darke who are men of high authority in this particular branch of study.

[16] 'Studies on the Genetic Determination of Homosexuality', *Journal of Nervous and Mental Diseases*, Vol. 92 (1940), p. 55.  T. Lang.

Even if a high familial incidence could be demonstrated, a genetic conclusion would be vitiated in many cases by the identity among brothers of environmental conditions which might also be the sole cause, or a contributory cause, of their homosexual condition.

# CHAPTER FOUR

# Hormonal Theory—Indirect and Direct Methods

~~~~~~~~~~~~~~~~~~~~~~~~~~~~~~~~~~~~~~~~~~~~~~~~~~~~

THE hormonal theory presents another aspect of the evidence for the biological, innate character of homosexuality. The upholders of this theory claim that hormonal imbalance is in varying degrees the cause of homosexuality. The homosexual is considered to be a male with the hormones and consequent sexual direction and urges of a female. Their therapy would consist mainly in hormonal injections to restore the balance of power, in so far as the workings of the ductless glands are considered to play an important, if not the dominant, role in the causation of the homosexual propensity.

*The hormonal theory* is a supposed development of the chromosomal theory, and is claimed to lead to a confirmation of the Third Sex claim for homosexuals. Havelock Ellis, stressing the importance of hormonal factors, sees homosexuality as

"the result of a quantitative disharmony between the male and female sex-determining factors. Being part of the hereditary constitution of the individual, it is inborn, likely to become more pronounced as development proceeds, and in the higher mammals, to manifest itself in the psychic sphere. . . . We may not know exactly what sex is; but we

47

do know that it is mutable, with the possibility of one sex being changed into the other sex. . . . We begin to come closer to the actual mechanism by which intersexuality is produced when we turn again to the action of the hormones. We may view these as taking up the guidance of the sex process after the influence of the initial sex-chromosomes, XX or XY, has been exhausted.  The somatic, or general, tissues of the body possess the potency of developing the characters of either sex under the special complex of sex-hormones which they receive.  The ovary . . . does not at any early stage exert any marked influence upon the soma, the female development being seemingly innate, though the developed female sex-equipment depends on the sex-hormones for its maintenance.  Male differentiation, on the other hand, requires the male testicular hormone for its development. Thus the female represents . . . the neutral form which the soma assumes in the absence of the male sex-hormone.  When the male hormone appears later than usual, some form of intersexuality thus results, and the later its appearance, the more femaleness there is in the result."[1]

Therefore, in Havelock Ellis' theory, if the male hormone is absent too long in the male XY sex-chromosome complex, or appears too early in the female XX chromosome structure, the resulting effect will be bodies with sexual characteristics of the opposite sex, and consequent homosexual or lesbian tendencies.

While not considering the presence of secondary sexual characteristics as absolutely essential to explain homosexuality, Havelock Ellis held that,

' apart from such measurable differences, there can be little doubt that certain individuals, in organic structure, and probably as a result of unusual hormonic balance, possess a

[1] *Psychology of Sex*, p. 166-7.

special aptitude to experience sexual satisfaction with persons of their own sex. . . . We seem justified in looking upon inversion as a congenital anomaly. . . . It is a variation doubtless due to imperfect sexual differentiation. Congenital sexual inversion is thus akin to a biological variation."[2]

Those who attempt to prove the hormonal causality of homosexuality proceed either *indirectly* by showing that the cause of the homosexual propensity must be attributed to the secondary female characteristics, which in turn is due to a preponderance of female hormones, or *directly* by linking causally hormonal imbalance and the direction of the homosexual drive. Taking each method in turn we turn our attention firstly to the *indirect* method.

Two sets of hormones have been invoked to explain homosexuality, androgens (male hormones) and oestrogens (female hormones). Androgens are said to cause the deep male voice, beard, pubic hair and other secondary male sexual characteristics. Oestrogens are held to be responsible for the development of the female sexual organs at puberty and inaugurate the menstrual cycle. It is generally believed that male and female hormones are present in either sex after the age of six, and there has been great speculation as to their influence on the soma and psyche of the growing child.

Rare cases of women suffering from tumour of the suprarenal gland have been reported, in which the secretion from the suprarenal gland[3] of an excess of male hormones has caused in these women:

---

[2] *Ibid.*, p. 168.
[3] The suprarenal gland secretes male hormones. " The cases of suprarenal tumour . . . are virtually museum pieces." ' Hormone Treatment; Treatment and Prevention.' *They Stand Apart*, p. 128.

"growth of beard, regression of the breasts and growth of the clitoris with alleged associated homosexual tendencies developing simultaneously."[4]

The administration of female hormones to men causes the fatty tissue of the chest to develop and inhibits sexual desire. Therefore, there is clear evidence, says Dr. Neustatter, "from experimental and clinical observation, that physical and sexual characteristics are dependent on endocrine function".[5]

The criticism of the theory under consideration is based primarily on the British Medical Association's Report which enumerates three experiments: Walker and Strauss (1945); Armstrong (1955); Swyer (1954).

*Walker and Strauss*, whose findings are the earliest of the three, stress the fact that even the most masculine homosexuals exhibited, or tended to exhibit, some slight traces of secondary sexual characteristics of the opposite sex. From their examinations they concluded that

"there is much to suggest that it depends primarily on a lack of balance between the various glands of internal secretion".[6]

*C. N. Armstrong*, in an article on the various 'Extreme Anomalies of Sex Variants',[7] which he treated professionally, chooses seven cases of which two are passive

---

[4] *Ibid.*, p. 71. Dr. Neustatter holds that tumour of the suprarenal gland causes precocious sexual development in children.

[5] *Ibid.*, p. 71.

[6] *Homosexuality and Prostitution*, p. 27.

[7] 'Diversities of Sex'. *British Medical Journal*, Vol. 1, (May, 1951) pp. 1173-7. C. N. Armstrong, M.D., F.R.C.P., D.P.H., Physician, Royal Victoria Infirmary, Newcastle upon Tyne, and Queen Elizabeth Hospital and Bensham General Hospital, Gateshead.

homosexuals with very marked feminine physical characteristics. As a result of his investigations carried out on
these extreme types of homosexuals, he feels:

> "the only contribution I have to make is that recently I
> have had several passive male homosexuals referred to me
> for an endocrine opinion, and in each instance I have been
> able to recognize certain female characteristics".[8]

*Swyer* confirms Armstrong's view with regard to
eunuchoidal passive homosexuals, but confines endocrinological influence to that type alone. He hold that:

> "The one possible variety of homosexuality which may be
> casually related to androgen deficiency in eunuchoidal
> patients is the passive type."[9]

But this does not avail for the common type of homosexuality, as there are "relatively rare instances"[10] of this
kind, namely, the eunuchoidal passive homosexual.

It may be legitimately concluded from the British
Medical Report that the only attempted link between an
excess of female hormones, secondary female sexual
characteristics and homosexuality in the male homosexual
is claimed for the eunuchoidal passive type. He is a rare
specimen and the exception among those who are homosexually orientated, hence experimentation in this sphere
cannot be of much practical utility in dealing with the
problem of homosexuality as a whole. Nevertheless it is
encouraging to notice that homosexuals of this unusual

[8] *Ibid.*, p. 1176.
[9] 'The Endocrinological Aspect,'—*The Practitioner*, 172. (April 1954),
p. 376. G. I. M. Swyer, D.M., D.Phil., M.R.C.P. Consultant Endocrinologist,
Dept. of Obstetrics and Gynaecology, University College Hospital.
[10] *Ibid.*, p. 377.

type may respond beneficially to clinical treatment.. Even where it is proved that the 'intersexual' state is due to hormonal imbalance, as in these rare cases, the Report admits that the psyche may not share the same intersexuality. Apart from the vague general statement that

> "doctors have noticed some homosexual persons have physical characteristics which indicate either a lack of normal virile features, or the positive presence of female ones".[11]

the Report admits that

> "the emotional characteristics may be dissociated from the physical ones, so that it is difficult to assess their significance. Moreover, there is no direct proof of their [secondary] sexual characteristics being determined by large abnormal quantities of known hormones".[12]

The Report admits elsewhere that "many homosexuals, some might say the majority, are very virile in their physical aspect".[13]

At this stage we have arrived at a suitable point to consider the homosexual who in varying degrees has feminine characteristics and dimensions in *body-build*. A homosexual may have a female body-build, but it would be wrong to conclude that his homosexuality was caused by his feminine physique. It is an accepted fact that many undoubted heterosexuals have as feminine a body structure as many known homosexuals. So the same feminine

[11] *Homosexuality and Prostitution*, p. 27.
[12] *Ibid.*, p. 29.
[13] *Ibid.*, p. 27.

structure, which is claimed as the cause of homosexuality
in one, does not induce a homosexual propensity in the
other. In fact, if body and emotion are inseparably connected, then such female characteristics should cause
homosexuality. It must not be forgotten that this book
concerns itself with males whose primary sexual characteristics are of the male species. Armstrong's 'extreme
cases' tend very much to the hermaphrodite. We are not
dealing with a genetic female who, because of secondary
sexual male characteristics, is thought to be male, because
her attraction for men would be heterosexual, and outside
the scope of the present work.

It is relatively important to decide whether or not
homosexuals have, in fact, a more female body-build than
heterosexuals, bearing in mind that group findings are of
little use in detecting the cause of homosexuality in any
particular case, except merely to offer an indication of a
possible cause. Some writers find proof of the hormonal
theory in the anthropological difference between the
measurements of the body-build of groups of homosexuals
and groups of heterosexuals, but

> "these differences are too slight to substantiate the theory
> that homosexuality is an intersex state between man and
> woman, because the mean of measurements for the male
> homosexual seems much closer to the male norm than
> to the female norm. The mean refers, of course, to a
> group".[14]

It is not disputed that some homosexuals are effeminate
in physique, but it is impossible to correlate causally body-
build and psychic outlook. It is now an accepted pheno-

[14] 'Homosexuality', *Psychiatry and Catholicism*, pp. 384-5.

menon that while it is not rare to find homosexuals with secondary sexual characteristics of the other sex, it is still less rare to find males with feminine physiques who are perfectly normal in the heterosexual direction of their sexual drive.[15]

Many consider that the homosexual is a 'pansy', with a female carriage of the arm and head, effeminate in speech and tastes, but this is often more the result of upbringing and environment than the effect of a female physique. Some male prostitutes adopt a 'female pose' to attract customers, and the majority of these are bisexuals or heterosexuals. It seems wrong to hold, that there is always a physical constitutional element determining a feminine attitude to the complete exclusion of environment. Indeed, if such men engage in homosexual practices, it may well be that they are attractive to genuine homosexuals, and may drift into an environment where there is opportunity for such sexual expressions, rather than for normal heterosexual acts, from which their feminine upbringing, and not their body-build, has excluded them. Certainly the recent medical report by Hemphill is emphatic in its denial of marked effeminacy as a general characteristic of homosexuals.[16]

The basis of the *indirect* method lies in its attempt to correlate feminine physical characteristics and hormonal imbalance with the implication that the genetic sex is opposed to the primary body-build, and follows the secondary female sexual characteristics. Yet "although in rare diseases, genetical sex may not agree with secondary

[15] 'Psychiatrist and Homosexual', *New Problems in Medical Ethics*, p. 70.
[16] 'A Factual Study of Male Homosexuality'. *British Medical Journal*, (June 7th, 1958), pp. 1317-23. R. E. Hemphill, M.D., D.P.M., A. Leitch, M.D., D.P.M., and J. R. Stuart, M.B., D.P.M.

sexual characteristics", says the British Medical Association's Report, "there seems no reason to believe that the common types of homosexuality have a genetic basis of this kind".[17] Neither must it be forgotten that the precocious appearance of homosexual tendencies in effeminate homosexuals rests on the testimony of homosexuals themselves, who may desire to find a justification for their lives, or attempt to convince the psychiatrist of the uselessness of any therapy. The only conclusion that may be drawn as regards the *indirect* method then is that it is an unproved hypothesis and cannot influence the moral judgement on the homosexual condition.

Consequent on the rejection of the indirect proof of the hormonal theory, there remains the *direct* method, which attempts to relate directly and causally the homosexual condition and an excess of female hormones. The tendency in medical circles has been to equate sexual *activity* with the *quantity* of hormones in the human body. One can see that it is an easy step for many doctors to go further, and equate the *direction* of the sexual drive with the *quality* of the preponderant hormones. In this case, there should be a high ratio of oestrogen or female hormones in homosexuals, which would be said to be the ultimate determining factor of their sexual abnormality. If the common or frequent type of homosexuality was due to hormonal imbalance, then castration should be the common cure to procure a cessation of sexual activity, and the injection of male hormones should direct the sexual drive into heterosexual channels.

Swyer, quoted in the British Medical Association's Report, is extremely

[17] *Homosexuality and Prostitution*, p. 26.

"critical of endocrinological theories in relation to homosexuality".[18] "It is now well established," he claims, "that
the capacity for sexual response, even to the point of
orgasm, is possessed by children of a very tender age.
Since these children have no effective amounts of circulating
sex hormones, it is quite clear that their capacity to respond
to sexual stimuli is not dependant upon the availability of
sex hormones".[19]

*Swyer denies the equation of sexual activity and the
quantity of sex hormones,* and bases his rejection mainly
on the observed sexual activity of adolescent boys and
girls.

"Comparison of the development of sexual behaviour in
adolescent boys and girls serves still further to underline the
complexity of the problem. In boys, a tremendous upsurge
of sexual ability, as indicated by frequency of ejaculation
from various stimuli, occurs at the time of puberty, and
thereafter shows a slow but steady decline. In girls, on the
other hand, a very different pattern obtains. . . . The
increase in sexual ability, as reflected by frequency of
arousal, whether or not it be to the point of orgasm, shows
only a slow increase over the period of adolescence and continues steadily in this way until a peak of activity is reached
around the age of thirty."

From all this Swyer concludes:

"It is thus quite impossible to regard the development of
sexual behaviour in the two sexes as the direct result of the
production of sex hormones, since the levels of male hormones in the male, and female hormones in the female

[18] 'Endocrine Factors'—*Homosexuality and Prostitution,* p. 27.
[19] 'Homosexuality: The Endocrinological Aspects', *The Practitioner,*
Vol. 127, p. 374.

rise more or less comparably at puberty, whilst the ensuing patterns of sexual behaviour are so vastly different. We must therefore conclude that the development of sexual responsiveness in the two sexes is dependent more upon psychological conditioning and availability of sexual outlets, than upon the levels of circulating hormones."[20]

Further light is thrown on the relationship between hormones and homosexual activity when we consider the question whether or not *castration* is an effective cure for the reduction or cessation of sexual activity among the majority, or at least a great number, of homosexuals? The answer supplied by the British Medical Association's Report is in the negative.

"The committee does not recommend castration as a method of treating homosexuality, although it has been adopted in certain continental countries. As with oestrogen treatment, castration is very effective in those cases in which it is adopted, though the proportion of cases suitable for this method is small. . . . Oestrogen treatment can always be abandoned without permanent effect on the patient, but a radical treatment such as castration could only be considered if it were almost invariably effective. There is moreover, some doubt whether castration always causes a cessation of sex drive."[21] Swyer also confirms this doubt when he claims: "it is equally well known that surgical castration of adult males may affect neither libido nor potency, so that once again, even in the absence of testicular androgens, sexuality remains unaffected".[22]

[20] *Ibid.*, p. 374.
[21] 'Forms of Treatment: Castration', *Homosexuality and Prostitution*, p. 48.
[22] 'Role of Sex Hormones in the Development of Sexual Behaviour', *The Practitioner*, Vol. 172, p. 374.

Dr. Neustatter, whose whole bias seems to be towards establishing a hormonal basis for homosexuality, is forced to concede that while castration may effect a decrease of desire, this is not destroyed altogether.[23]  These is no absolute guarantee that such a reduction will be affected in a particular case, and even in this case, other homosexual offences may occur again.[24]  Therefore it is legitimate to conclude that something other than hormones is responsible for the sex drive in the majority of homosexuals.

Is hormonal influence to be discarded completely as an explanation of sexual activity?  It is as wrong to deny all influence as it was wrong to assert all.  It is false to assert that the majority of homosexuals are such because of an excess quantity of female hormones, yet it seems that there exists a small group who would benefit by hormonal treatment, but these are the exceptions.

Before attempting *the investigation of hormonal imbalance and the direction of the homosexual drive* it is important to stress that the main case for the hormonal theory lies in its effort to prove that the homosexual is really an intersexual whose homosexual propensity derives from his secondary female sexual characteristics which in turn are the outcome of excess female hormones in his constitutional make-up.  Marañòn holds homosexuality to be an intersexual state, yet                                   .

"offering this peculiarity—that the functional trouble is much more intense than the anatomical disturbance, unlike all the other intersexual conditions studied in Medicine.

[23] 'Treatment and Prevention, Hormone Treatment'.  *They Stand Apart*, p. 128.
[24] *Homosexuality and Prostitution*, p. 48.

This predominance of the functional alteration of libido disturbance shows us, on the other hand, the primordial role which we must attribute in its pathogeny to the cooperation of psychological factors. . . . The very fact that homosexuality corresponds in general to the slight and not to the intense forms of morphological homosexuality is very significant from the point of view of their respective relative independence. . . . If hormonal bisexuality is a necessary condition for the development of homosexuality, it is nevertheless not sufficient to produce homosexuality ".[25]

If female hormones were the sole determinant of the homosexual direction of the sexual drive then one would expect to find an endocrine imbalance in homosexuals. The British Medical Association admits that "no conclusive data have been provided",[26] and is keenly aware that

"the absence of an established correlation between major endocrine disorders and homosexual behaviour has been used as an argument against an endocrine basis for homosexuality".[27]

The Association's Report, therefore, does not attempt to defend the theory that sufficient evidence exists for the correlation of endocrine imbalance and the direction of the homosexual drive. Accepting the fact that no sufficient proof exists, it explains this as due to the fact "that endocrinologists have not concerned themselves with the abnormal sexual behaviour of their patients", but have confined themselves in their research work to establishing

[25] *New Problems in Medical Ethics*, p. 80.
[26] 'Endocrine Factors', *Homosexuality and Prostitution*, p. 28.
[27] *Ibid.*, p. 28.

a relationship between "feminine characteristics with a relative excess of urinary oestrogens in relation to urinary androgens"[28] in homosexual patients. Even in this limited field, as we shall see later in this chapter, they have failed to obtain conclusive data.

Cases will arise where the homosexual has a high-oestrogen low-androgen ratio, but it would be wrong to conclude that this unbalanced hormonal ratio is the cause of his homosexuality. Dr. Neustatter is forced to admit:

> "When it comes to establishing any relationship between these hormones and the direction of the sexual desire, there is unfortunately little evidence."[29]

Further light on the problem, whether or not homosexuality is associated with an excess of female hormones is shown by a consideration of *certain medical cases which are known to be associated with the production of abnormal amounts of hormones*. If incidences of homosexuality are not found in these cases or, if present before these conditions arose, do not show an increase, then the evidence against the necessary connection between endocrine imbalance and homosexuality would seem irrefutable.

For male patients suffering from cancer of the prostate gland, the medical treatment given is an administration of female hormones, by which the androgen-oestrogen ratio is greatly altered, and yet there is no evidence of any increased tendency to homosexuality.

> "In patients suffering from the male climacteric eunuchism and eunuchoidism, there is absolutely no increased in-

[28] *Ibid.*, p. 28.
[29] 'Homosexuality; Incidence and Causation. The Sexual Hormones'. *They Stand Apart*, p. 71.

cidence of homosexuality as compared with that in the general population."[30]

*Hormonal therapy* also, as a general remedy, is considered to be *a failure.*[31] Many doctors attempted to transform male homosexuals into heterosexuals by implanting into their tissues the gonads of a normal man.[32]

"These efforts, at first welcomed with enthusiasm, proved to be an illusion; the operation scored only mild success when it was preceded by castration."[33] Some doctors discovered that if they injected their homosexual patients with gonadotropins which should theoretically increase the number of male and decrease the female hormones, the reverse occurred. The drive, far from changing its homosexual direction, was strengthened, and the tendency to commit homosexual acts increased.[34]

[30] " Artificial alteration of the androgen-oestrogen ratio is now commonly encountered when patients with carcinoma of the prostate are treated with large doses of stilboestrol. If such an altered ratio had any significance in the genesis of homosexuality, one would have expected to have encountered numerous instances among such patients. None has been reported. In precisely the same way the development of androgen-secreting tumours in women, or the administration of large doses of androgen (as, for example, in the palliative treatment of carcinoma of the breast) does not lead to any alteration in the direction of their libido." ' Homosexuality: The Endocrinological Aspects' *The Practitioner*, 172 (1954), p. 376.

[31] " The use of sex hormones in the treatment of homosexuality is mainly disappointing." *Ibid.*, p. 377.

[32] " If it is true that homosexuality is determined by the relative predominance of the hormones of the opposite sex, it might be expected that the homosexual would be cured of his disorder by the transplantation of the gonads of a normal individual into his issues, or by the administration of endocrine extract." *Ibid.*, p. 377.

[33] ' Homosexuality: Therapy'. *Psychiatry and Catholicism*, p. 388.

[34] *Journal of Clinical Endocrinology.* (1944), Vol. 4, p. 540. S. J. Glass and R. H. Johnson. " In the vast majority of males who show predominantly homosexual tendencies, however, androgen treatment serves merely to increase the libido, which still remains homosexual in outlook." Swyer, *The Practitioner*, 172 (1954), p. 377.

Is medical treatment, then, of any value in the therapy of homosexuals? It may be especially useful in particular cases in helping to break the vicious circle of repeated homosexual practices, and aiding the homosexual to overcome his obsession, thus gaining confidence in his ability to control his passions.[35]

"The drugs mostly used in the treatment of homosexuals are the oestrogens, (stilboestrol, ethinyl oestradiol, etc.) which produce temporary cessation or diminution of sexual desire in most subjects. When the drug is stopped, normal sexual feeling returns."[36]

These drugs may be used as a semi-permanent treatment in those who are old, yet may be found to be of little value for young people.[37]

"It is most effective in a small group of patients who are very highly sexed, and with some of these the dose may be adjusted to reduce, rather than suppress, sexual feelings."[38]

Just as the success of antabuse for alcoholics depends on the guarantee that the patient is taking it continually, so also with stilboestrol.[39] Yet the psychopaths and those

[35] "In some who have been repeatedly punished and despair of avoiding further imprisonment, the drug may break a vicious circle and allow them to give up homosexual associations; when the treatment is abandoned later, their situation has greatly improved." *Homosexuality and Prostitution*, p. 48.

[36] *Ibid.*, p. 48.

[37] "It is useful . . . as a semi-permanent treatment in older patients in whom there is no contra-indication to severe limitation of sexual life. . . . Young people are rarely suitable for drug treatment unless the outlook is very poor." *Ibid.*, p. 48.

[38] *Ibid.*, p. 48.

[39] Stilboestrol to be effective must be taken at least on alternate days. This disadvantage might be overcome by 'depot implants' in which a subcutaneous pellet would be sufficient for about a month.

who need it most are the least liable to continue the treatment faithfully, and the only safe check seems to be that they put on weight.

The only possible type of homosexual group in which hormonal treatment seems efficacious enough to change the homosexual direction into normal heterosexual channels, is of the rare passive eunuchoidal homosexual, for whom, even Swyer admits, "male hormone treatment may prove completely successful".[40] This is confirmed by L. A. Lurie, among others, who claims that passive eunuchoidal homosexuals alone respond to sex-hormone treatment through the medium of injecting intra-muscularly testosterone propionate, and other extracts.[41] Dr. Neustatter, too, makes the following cogent remarks:

"the general consensus of opinion", he concedes, "is that the role of endocrine treatment is confined to sexually undeveloped types who show a passive homosexual disposition", but, "such cases are rare".[42] "One must conclude, therefore, that present-day knowledge does not allow it to be said that any known sexual hormones cause homosexuality. . . . All that can be said is that hormones which produce known sexual characteristics have no effect in regard to the direction of the sexual impulse".[43]

It is relative at this stage to consider whether or not the *urinary output of homosexuals* shows any endocrine imbalance. Since people carry in their blood both androgen and oestrogen, many investigators have tried to

[40] *The Practitioner*, 172 (1954), p. 377. Swyer considers "normal sexual feelings and abilities" (p. 374), as completely successful treatment.
[41] 'The Endocrine Factor in Homosexuality', *The American Journal of Medical Science*. Vol. 208, 1944, pp. 176-86.
[42] *They Stand Apart*, p. 128.
[43] *Ibid.*, p. 72.

find a support for the hormonal causality of homosexuality by measuring the ratio of androgen and oestrogen in the urinary output of groups of homosexual and heterosexual people. They hope to show that there is an endocrine imbalance in the homosexual group. Some, like Dr. Leonard Simpson have then tried to correlate the relative excess of urinary oestrogens with secondary female sexual characteristics. Others, such as Neustadt and Myerson, in their study did not confine themselves to the physical build, but rather their primary purpose was to relate excess urinary oestrogens with actual homosexual practices and tendencies. The British Medical Report is more concerned with relating hormonal excess in groups of homosexuals with female sexual characteristics, than in directly relating such an excess, if proved to be present, with actual homosexual tendencies. It is again more the *indirect* approach.

Apart from the work of Armstrong and Swyer, which has already been examined, the only other research work mentioned in the Report is that at present being conducted by Dr. Simpson himself in collaboration with consultants and general practitioners. Since the relationship between homosexuality and secondary female sexual characteristics has already been discussed, the value of this research is restricted. Certain female features are found to be present in varying degrees in the cases so far examined by Dr. Simpson, ranging from " 10% to 50%, according to the groups studied, and perhaps varying with the observers ".[44] This difference is too great to be of any value specifically, if the result finally shows that homosexuals as a group only differ slightly from heterosexuals.

[44] *Homosexuality and Prostitution*, p. 29.

Glass, Deul and Wright (1940) conducted a similar investigation, and concluded that there was an altered androgen-oestrogen ratio in homosexuals as a group.[45] Kinsey (1941) corrected the mathematical errors in their paper, and then went on to state:

"one is not warranted in concluding that the relatively small differences in averages between two such small groups are significant when successive samples from single individuals show from seven to fifty times as much difference ".[46]

Their method of sampling also did not escape condemnation by Kinsey. By one method of sampling they found that the homosexual had more androgen than the normal group, whereas by another method there was less androgen. Such large standard errors destroy any conclusions that may be drawn from such investigations.

Neustadt and Myerson examined twenty-nine homosexuals, and of these found that in twenty-five cases there was an endocrine imbalance. However convincing this may seem, the numbers examined are too small for a problem of such magnitude. Their findings may serve as a support for some future research, whenever it is undertaken on a much larger scale.[47] Swyer quotes many who have carried out similar enquiries, and he says that:

[45] 'Sex Hormone Studies in male homosexuals.' Endocrinology, 26, (1940), pp. 590-4.
[46] Journal of Clinical Endocrinology, Vol. 1, p. 424.
[47] 'Quantitative Sex Hormone Studies in Homosexuality. Childhood and Various Neuropsychiatric Disturbances.' American Journal of Psychiatry, Vol. 97, pp. 524-51.

"it may be stated categorically that no convincing demonstrations of endocrine imbalance in 'homosexuals' have been forthcoming ".[48]

Among the most recent works was that undertaken by Garrone and Mutrux who studied a group of fifty patients with anomalies of sexual behaviour including homosexuality. Their work is described in the annotations of the British Medical Journal as:

"a careful and extensive study, which leads to the now almost overwhelming evidence against endocrine causes, and therefore for psychological causes of these behavioural disorders ".[49]

The daily urinary output of these patients did not differ from that of normal men of corresponding ages.

"The conclusion was therefore reached that this group of patients did not provide any evidence of endocrine disturbance such as could account for their disordered sexual behaviour."[50]

Their findings are corroborated by Hemphill and his colleagues who state quite categorically from their examination of sixty-four prisoners that

"there was no evidence of endocrine abnormality or marked effeminacy, and the urinary excretions of 17-ketosteroids and the androgen-oestrogen ratios were of no diagnostic value ".[51]

---

[48] *The Practitioner*, 172 (1954), p. 375.
[49] 'Endocrine and Disordered Sexual Behaviour', *British Medical Journal*, (March 9th, 1957), 574.
[50] *Ibid.*, p. 574.
[51] 'A Factual Study of Male Homosexuals'. *British Medical Journal*, (June 7th, 1958), p. 1322.

It is logical, therefore, in the light of available medical evidence that we should reject the *direct* method as the main causal influence of the common type of homosexuality. *The hormonal theory as a whole* affords little or no basis on to which to construct moral principles, and it is beyond question that the general pattern of homosexuality is chiefly due to something other than hormonal imbalance.

# CHAPTER FIVE

# Familial Incidence. Conclusion of Medical Case

~~~~~~~~~~~~~~~~~~~~~~~~~~~~~~~~~~~~~~~~~~~~~~~~~~~~~~~~

THE indirect and direct methods having contributed little to establish the case for the constitutional character of homosexuality, other investigations into the familial incidence of homosexuality have tried to prove that some unknown physical element is the determining factor in the origin of homosexuality. They claim for example, that homosexuality runs in families, so that it can be said to be inherited. Before considering any statistics, it is necessary to weigh the value of any such findings in the light of the following facts, most of them admitted by the British Medical Association, as governing such investigations and thereby limiting the number of valid inferences that may be made.[1]

It is very difficult to prove the genetic basis in any given case, or even for a group as *the problem of homosexuality is very much influenced by environment*, especially in familial groups, where valid inferences as to the physical elements involved are greatly reduced. It seems generally agreed that homosexuality is largely functional.[2] Again

---

[1] 'The Case for a Genetic Basis', *Homosexuality and Prostitution*, p. 24.
[2] "Homosexuality is in fact an undesirable trait for precise genetical study because its character is complex, it does not show clear segregation, and it is much influenced by environment." *Ibid.*, p. 24.

the character of homosexuality is so complex in its nature that in the vast majority of cases it does not seem traceable to any single determining factor; e.g., so far in the medical field we only know of the *rare cases* of eunuchoidal passive homosexuals who seem in large part, if not completely, physically determined to homosexuality.

Statistics as such may be valid for a group, but cannot be claimed as responsible for homosexuality in any particular case. All that might be proved from statistics is that homosexuals as a group are to some extent determined by heredity, without thereby inferring that *this particular patient* is hereditarily determined. There may be some constitutional element in some types of homosexuality, but that would not mean that everyone in this group, or this particular homosexual, is an inborn homosexual, i.e., that his homosexual propensity is chiefly due to physical causes.

Homosexuality by itself is rarely the subject of clinical study, and it is generally only when it is accompanied by some psychopathic disorder, which is studied for itself, that homosexuality is brought to the notice of the doctor.[3] It is difficult to segregate it from these psychopathic disorders, of which it has come to be regarded as a symptom. The conclusions, therefore, as to homosexuality's constitutional basis are only by implication,[4] when it is grouped with these psychopathic disorders.

Homosexuals are generally very secretive about their abnormality and are extremely unwilling to 'let anyone

[3] "Indeed, it may be that only when homosexuality is associated with an intercurrent psychopathic condition does it constitute a clinical problem." *Ibid.*, p. 24.

[4] "In so far as it can be regarded as a symptom of psychopathic disorder, its genetics may be studied by implication when the familial incidence of a more inclusive disorder is being investigated." *Ibid.*, p. 24.

into their secret'. Those who do volunteer information
about their condition may try to justify their moral
theorizing by complaining that they are made that way
through no fault of their own; that homosexuality is a
physical irresistible force which holds them in its power.
Often anti-social and subjective, their testimony is very
definitely open to suspicion.

Doctors compile their statistics from 'volunteered information' and from 'clinical studies', generally of
neurotics and other disturbed personalities.

"The late Havelock Ellis had to base his estimates of
incidence of the disorder largely on clinical experience."[5]

These statistics depreciate in validity if they are to serve
as a basis for a general estimate of the homosexual
world as doctors see a selective group rather than a cross-
section of homosexuals. When homosexuals do seek
advice from a doctor it is more often than not because
they are in trouble with the police, or are on the verge
of a serious nervous collapse. Many homosexuals so order
their lives that they avoid conflict with the law, and there
are very few who can afford the long and expensive course
of psychiatric treatment. The figures given by criminal
and clinical doctors, psychoanalysts and psychiatrists, are
composed mainly from these extreme cases, and are no
infallible guarantee or guide to the 'normal' or common
types of homosexual.

[5] 'The Medical Aspects. Introduction', *They Stand Apart*, p. 67. This
statement is supported by Curran and Parr, the former being a member of
the Wolfenden Committee.
    'Homosexuality: An Analysis of 100 Male Cases Seen in Private Practice',
*British Medical Journal* (April 6th, 1957) pp. 797-801.

Finally, it must be said that the extent of the problem is not commensurate with the amount of available evidence. The study of homosexuality involves such personal prejudices, that the results are often a reflection of an approving or disapproving 'pre-determined' attitude to homosexuals in general on the part of the statistician, rather than an objective critical analysis of the scientific observations warranting certain conclusions, which very often they do not get.[6]

In the light of the foregoing statements we shall now examine the most conclusive statistics available up to the present. The only figures available come from *two main sources*; *implication from psychopathic disorders, and familial incidences of homosexuality*. Because homosexuality, as we have said, is rarely a clinical case unless it is associated with an intercurrent psychopathic condition, there are no figures for homosexuality itself as such in the works of Slater and Brown, quoted by the British Medical Association Report. Their investigations serve merely to indicate whether or not there is some genetical background in most types of mental disorder. To apply their figures to homosexuality is, in a sense, to presume that homosexuality is a mental disorder. Even if it were, then their figures are only valid by implication.

Felix Brown's contribution is enhanced by the fact that he admits that he had a "prejudice against the signifi-

---

[6] " The results of any forms of treatment are notoriously difficult to assess, and are inclined to give rise to passionate controversy in most fields of medicine; the field of homosexuality is no exception to the rule. Probably, owing to the difficulty of assessing results and obtaining adequate follow-ups, no figures of results appear to exist. The field is thus wide open to expression of clinical opinions, which vary from the very cautious to the incredibly optimistic and probably more accurately reflect the personality of their sponsors than the reliability of the results." ' The Medical Aspects. Introduction ', *They Stand Apart*, p. 67.

cance of heredity in the psychoneuroses ",[7] and his study makes no attempt to belittle the importance of environment. Yet after personal investigations he is forced to the conclusion, that even though it is impossible at present to separate completely environment and heredity,

> "nevertheless from such evidence as we have, heredity plays quite as important a part as environment in the development of psychoneuroses ".[8]

His studies were comprehensive in so far as his patients were not confined to one social class.[9]  It is interesting to note that

> "the environment in which these psychoneuroses developed was the peace-time environment, and the stresses were the familiar ones of family and sexual relationships, and work difficulties ".[10]

Dividing his patients into three classes he concluded that there was 'true heredity' in 15% of the anxiety states, while the figure for hysteria and obsessional states was 7%.

Brown's findings were confirmed by Dr. Eliot Slater's later works, but the latter emphasized the extreme difficulty of tackling such a problem, due to environment playing such a tremendous part in familial influence.  He also admitted that the genetical component is a very indeterminate one in "the groups of psychopathic or

[7] 'Heredity in Psychoneuroses', *Proceedings of the Royal Society of Medicine*, Vol XXXV, 1942, pp. 785-90.

[8] *Ibid.*, p. 790.

[9] Brown took his subjects from the "Out-Patients Department of Guy's Hospital and the Cassel Hospital, so that cases are not confined to one social class ", *Ibid.*, p. 786.

[10] *Ibid.*, p. 790.

neurotic conditions, or of neuroses".[11] Yet Slater does hold that in varying degrees there is some genetical background in most types of mental disorder.[12]

A much stronger case is forthcoming when we examine *the familial incidences of homosexuality*. Hirschfeld claimed that homosexuality was determined to a large extent by heredity, because he found more than one member of the same family was homosexual. He held that while it was not uncommon to find the father and son homosexual, it was quite a frequent occurrence to find homosexuality among pairs of brothers.

"The heredity of inversions is well-marked", writes Havelock Ellis, "though it has sometimes been denied; sometimes a brother and sister, a mother and son, an uncle and nephew, are both inverted even unknown to each other. I find this family or hereditary inversion in thirty-five per cent cases."[13]

"Kinsey criticizes these figures, and points out that it would need extraordinarily large numbers to prove anything, in view of the prevalence of homosexuality, and asserts that in fact there is no such proof."[14]

The difficulty in such studies, which must always be remembered, is to determine what influence environment exercises, as it alone could possibly account for all the

[11] *Homosexuality and Prostitution*, p. 24.
[12] 'The Neurotic Constitution. A statistical study of two thousand neurotic soldiers', *Journal of Neurotic Psychiatry*, Vol. 6 (1943) 1. E. Slater.
'A demographic study of the psychopathic population', *Ann. Eugen.* (Lond.), Vol. 12 (1944) 121. E. Slater.
'A heuristic theory of neurosis', *Journal of Neurotic Psychiatry*, Vol. 17 (1944), p. 49. E. Slater and P. Slater.
[13] *Psychology of Sex*, p. 169.
[14] 'The Medical Aspects. Incidence and Causation of Homosexuality. Hereditary and Constitutional Factors', *They Stand Apart*, p. 77.

cases of familial incidence where the children are brought up together. Some writers, too, find that the male homosexual tends to deviate towards scoring patterns characteristic of the opposite sex, so that a very feminine mother rears a very feminine son. Familial incidence is most inconclusive in affording support for a genetic background, and seems rather to strengthen the environmental theory.[15]

Henry's study of 40 male homosexuals is mentioned by the British Medical Association's Report. Of 51 male and 55 female sibs, he found that there were 6 homosexuals, 3 of either sex. Henry's sibs are not much more homosexual than the American people from whom they were drawn—if any reliability is to be placed on Kinsey's figures, 5·6% to 4%. The Report adds, however, that as regards Henry's study, "it is difficult to decide how much weight may be given to such a finding".[16]

Perhaps the strongest case for some constitutional element in the familial homosexuality is furnished by studies on *homosexual twins*. The investigation most often quoted was undertaken by Kallman in the United States, and appears to be the largest and most comprehensive of its kind. His investigation is of special interest in so far as he discovered that identical twins brought up under different circumstances became homosexual, unknown to each other. Yet this can be explained by the fact that the environment in the different surroundings was of such a nature as to foster a homosexual condition. In addition it must be remembered that these twins were

---

[15] *Sex and Personality*, L. M. Terman and C. C. Miles, (New York, 1936).
[16] *Homosexuality and Prostitution*, p. 25.

deprived of their natural parents, which is claimed to be one of the *environmental causes* of homosexuality.

Kallman noticed a great difference in the incidence of the homosexual pattern between uniovular and binovular twins.[17]

|  | High degree of Homosexuality | Some Degree | None | Total |
|---|---|---|---|---|
| Uniovular Twins | 31 | 13 | — | 44 |
| Binovular Twins | 2 | 11 | 38 | 51 |

In all the uniovular twins there was some degree of homosexuality, and in 70% they were practically exclusively homosexual. On the other hand, only about 4% of the binovular twins were homosexual to a high degree—the same as Kinsey's figures for the American population—while there is some homosexuality present in 25%, or a quarter of the number examined.

Apart from the general considerations governing all such statistical studies which we enumerated earlier, Kallman's investigation may have something to offer future research workers. It does seem to show some unknown physical background, and deserves closer medical examination if doctors are to attempt a diagnosis of the exact nature of the anomaly. The British Medical Association, commenting on these findings, holds that:

"The close similarity of uniovular twins suggests that certain genes lay down a potentiality which, in average circumstances, will lead to homosexuality in the person who possesses them. In peculiar circumstances, the geneti-

[17] Uniovular—a splitting in two of ONE ovum immediately after fertilization. Binovular—simultaneous fertilization of TWO ova. *Ibid.*, pp. 77-8. Uniovular twins have the same genetic structure or are identical twins, while binovular have different genetic structure and may be quite different from each other, e.g. of different sexes.

cal potentiality may be suppressed. Twin data are usually too circumscribed to give information about such eventualities or to help to identify the main causes of homosexuality in a given case which comes under observation. The marked disparity between uniovular and binovular twin pairs, however, fairly conclusively excludes the hypothesis of single gene determination. Whatever the genetical influences are, they must be complex."[18]

All the foregoing evidence submitted by the British Medical Association seems to destroy its own 'case for a genetic basis' of homosexuality. What little data there is tends, as we have seen, to be against the inborn character of the homosexual propensity. The two main hypotheses—namely, the chromosomal theory and the hormonal theory—which could establish the physical aspect of homosexuality, cannot be accepted, and must be rejected on available scientific evidence.

Do homosexuals form an intersex group? An answer in the affirmative without any scientific proof would no more stand than any other gratuitous assertion. Its answer and refutation could consist in an equally gratuitous denial. Our refusal to accept the chromosomal theory is based on scientific experiments approved by the British Medical Association itself. Since it may be lawfully objected that only two experiments are mentioned in the Report, we have not absolutely excluded the chromosomal theory. Future experiments may prove such an explanation to be the correct and only one, yet for the present it is an unscientific hypothesis. The onus of proving the medical constitutional character of homosexuality is with those who propound such a theory and demand its accept-

[18] *Homosexuality and Prostitution*, p. 26.

ance. *That they have failed to do so leads logically to its rejection.*

The hormonal explanation is equally inconclusive, and does not of itself alone involve the common type of homosexuality. This is clearly shown by the medically accepted fact that hormonal treatment is of little use therapeutically except in a small proportion of homosexuals. In some homosexuals secondary female sexual characteristics are found to be present, with an accompanying endocrine imbalance. But whatever scanty proof exists connecting causally these sexual characteristics and an excess of female hormones, there is even less, in fact none, to demonstrate the consequence of the homosexual propensity as due to the somatic condition. In fact there are no means available at present which could effect this latter proof.

Those who attempt to establish the constitutional character of homosexuality proceed by three ways in descending degrees of importance and availability of proof. (*a*) Secondary sexual characteristics of the opposite sex and endocrine imbalance. (*b*) Where this intersomatic condition is obviously lacking—as it is in the majority of homosexuals—then an endocrine imbalance is postulated as the cause of homosexuality. (*c*) Since this endocrine imbalance is unproved, then the chromosome complex is invoked, but this is the weakest of all, and is not only unproved, but unprovable in the present state of medical knowledge. *All three ways, as we have seen, have been rejected.*

It is possible that there may be some constitutional factors, involved in varying degrees in different homosexuals, which contribute to their homosexual propensity,

but there is no way of deciding what exactly they are, or
the extent of their influence.[19]    One fact is indisputable.
If homosexuality has any constitutional basis, then it is a
very slight one.   Homosexuals have normal erections and
emissions, so that it must be concluded by the upholders
of the hormonal theory that their sexual structure is
essentially normal.[20]   If homosexuality is written in the
soma, then present scientific knowledge and methods can
help us very little in reading its message.

However, even if it is shown that emotional factors are
the most predominant feature of homosexuality, they
must not be considered to be the only factors involved.

> "Medicine has come to look upon the human body as a
> mechanism of great precision, whose parts fit into each
> other and are naturally linked with each other."[21]

It is wrong to divorce the soma from the psyche, and in
assessing the role of the doctor in treating homosexuals
it is as well to remember that the individual homosexual's
psyche and soma interact and affect one another.   A
homosexual is not just an abnormal or immature 'body'
nor just a perverted 'soul'.

The need for a careful assessment of physical imbalance
is most clearly seen in the small class of physically deter-

---

[19] " With increased knowledge it may be possible to analyse and resolve
the so-called constitutional factors; they may, for example, really be the
expression of some physiological disfunction which as yet we do not understand.   If so, at present there is nothing that can be done about them."
'Hereditary and Constitutional Factors. Homosexuality. Incidence and
Causation', They Stand Apart, p. 77.

[20] That the vast majority of homosexuals have normal sex organs and
normal sex activity is generally admitted today.

[21] Catholic Documents XII, (July 1953).   Address of Pope Pius XII
to delegates attending the Fifth Congress of Psychotherapy and Clinical
Psychology.

mined homosexuals, described by Armstrong (p. 51) as eunuchoidal passives but who could also be called sexually immature from a physiological point of view. They obviously fall within the doctor's care, for he can supplement their deficiency of sex hormones and thus attempt to procure physiological sexual maturity. Even so, these cases will require help other than the doctor's, so that they may readjust themselves emotionally, especially in the formation of their approach to the opposite sex.

The doctor's assistance may also be required in the initial treatment of some hypersexed practising homosexuals of long standing to enable them to break the vicious circle of their evil habits. In such cases the doctor could diminish the sex urge directly by giving small doses of female sex hormones, or indirectly by giving a sedative. There is a great dearth of scientific research in the medical field. Nevertheless it is encouraging to note that during the course of a parliamentary debate of high level on the Wolfenden Report in November, 1958, the British Government through the Home Secretary promised to provide assistance and encouragement for further scientific researches into the problem. *At the moment, however, we believe that homosexuality is not basically a medical problem.*

# CHAPTER SIX

# The Homosexual and his Early Family Environment

THE inadequacy of the medical theories in their attempts to establish the constitutional character of homosexuality compels the investigator to look elsewhere for the etiological factors involved. By many psychiatrists, homosexuality is considered to be an abnormality traceable to the 'psyche' rather than the 'soma': a psychological instead of a physiological malady: a mental deviation and not a structural disturbance. This emphasis on the 'psyche' has led to a riot of conflicting opinions varying according to the school of thought of the psychiatrist. It would be impossible in the space of this short work to consider all these theories. Nevertheless, no work on homosexuality would be complete without an enumeration of those most often quoted in present-day psychology.

Freud considers homosexuality as primarily a reaction to an unresolved Oedipus complex. In the third or fourth year of an infant's life there is supposed to be an affective fixation on the parent of the opposite sex. When the child accepts his own sex completely then these tendencies will end in pure and affectionate tenderness. The boy will model himself on his father but, if anything goes wrong to disturb this normal cycle, a fixation may occur, thus giving rise to an affective inversion in which "the tender seduction is towards the father, the imitation is of the mother to whom the attachment will be intense and sometimes definitive ".[1] The son identifies himself with the mother and imitates her in everything, including her sexual life, so that "henceforward the sexual role which the infant will have to play can only be a female role ".[2]

Adler sees the whole problem of homosexuality in terms of dominance or submission within the family, and in the wider society. This theory may prove a useful line of enquiry in modern Western Society which emancipates woman and tends to stress her equality and masculinity. Adler holds that a child will tend to identify himself with the dominant parent of either sex. There is evidence also that one may rebel against the dominant parent or parent figure. In the same way a child may protect itself by submission to a dominant sibling of the same sex.

Jung equates homosexuality and role-rejection. The masculine and feminine elements (animus and anima) present in the human psyche, seek to balance each other. In the man the masculine side is conscious and the feminine exercises its activity in the unconscious. Independently of the sex of the individual, there is great variability in the conscious role played by the two elements. Thus men who have not liberated themselves from the 'Mother Anima' would be attracted to masculine women in the same way that women whose masculine side (the animus) is uppermost would be drawn to feminine men. The homosexual is in conflict in himself against this sensed

[1] *New Problems in Medical Ethics*, p. 81.
[2] *Ibid.*, p. 81.

awareness of the 'Mother Anima'—this is the motive of his role-rejection—and so reacts into homosexuality.

In this theory the life-process is a developmental one, and the unconscious teleology in the psyche strives among other things to balance the masculine and feminine in the self so that the integrated individual would be psychologically bisexual. This reconciling of opposites is supposed to take place only in middle life when the biological tasks are completed. In earlier adulthood proper role-identification is stressed, so that to each stage of life there is a corresponding role or function. Man's task is first to fulfil his social role as father, worker, husband: and woman's to be mother, helpmate, inspirer. When these roles are not accepted or fulfilled, various psychological ills may arise among which may be included homosexuality.

Gide's concept of homosexuality is as an effect of philosophical idealism. Among the ancient Greeks, philosophical idealism led them to the rejection of material values and exaltation of the spiritual, which it typified in their attitude to their wives and their extolling of friendship between males. Everything to do with sex and generation is rejected. Love for them is divorced from its familial context, and we in the West, intellectual heirs of the Greeks, still fall into the same emotional traps, which are the psychological outcome of this Greek Idealism.

While we do not accept the psychoanalytical theory of the universality of the homosexual component, yet there is a homosexual urge which varies quantitatively in certain persons. This varies also quantitatively in the same individual at different periods of his life. Grave harm has been done by looking on homosexuality as an 'all or none condition'. We feel that there is a certain mysterious ambivalence in the psychological and emotional outlook which does not necessarily correspond to physical sexual determination. This is probably the root cause of homosexuality, because as we have seen, the homosexually inclined are not more feminine in body-build than those who evince no homosexual attraction. This ambivalence is generally overcome in normal environmental and educational processes, so that eventually the mature individual is integrated with an emotional and psychological make-up harmonizing with his physical structure. Any abnormality will threaten this integration, and the results will vary with the individual. The homosexual is not possessed of an integrated personality and this we feel is generally traceable to abnormal environment affecting his constitutional background. Homosexuality is essentially an emotional malady, and in some cases the homosexual propensity seems determined without any advertence on the part of the subject, so that damage in varying degrees is effected before rational activity has begun.

We do not intend to examine each of these four theories in detail, nor to follow the intricate and complex meanings which through them are read into apparently inconsequential happenings. While we do not commit ourselves to the belief that their views are correct, yet in a limited way they help us to solve the enigma of homosexuality. Jung's theory seems the most acceptable, with the attempted balancing of the male and female elements in the human psyche, and the role rejection of the homosexual because he is in conflict against his sensed awareness of the 'Mother Anima'. His lack of emotional balance and the dominance of the female element in contradistinction to his male sex are common phenomena in the pattern of homosexuality.

Freud is justifiably criticized for his false theories on morality and his unacceptable concept of the essential composition of man. However, irrespective of the Oedipus-complex theory, he did uncover the fact that normal heterosexuality is accomplished mainly through the boy's modelling himself on his father. Case histories show clearly that when this father-son relationship is disturbed a not-infrequent result is homosexuality. Even the most casual investigator of the familial background of homosexuals is convinced that the abnormality is greatly influenced by the mother's dominant presence in the youth's emotional life, and the occurrence is too common to be reduced to the realms of coincidence.

Adler's theory of dominance and submission is equally well-established by case histories. Yet there is no denying that normal heterosexual males come from homes as equally dominated as those of homosexuals. There seems to be an unknown basic element in the human make-up which affects different people in completely different ways —the one to rebel and the other to submit.

Gide's theory has a limited application, confining itself to those homosexuals who find their deviation a source of intellectual and aesthetic inspiration. This attitude is found quite frequently in University coteries and among those who undertake certain professions. These homosexuals often use their deviation as an incentive to greater efforts in their various occupations, hoping thereby to demonstrate that their homosexuality is justifiable in view of the great gifts it bestows upon its adherents.

*Family environment, particularly in early years,* is now regarded as a crucial factor in a person's formation. It used to be a common fallacy that what happens in infancy does not matter much, and nowadays it is contended, with equal falsity, that a child of five years is *already* sexually determined. This latter theory would destroy the concept of personal moral responsibility for the origin of sexual states, as the sexual condition would be completely due to factors outside the conscious control of the individual. Yet it is true that even at this tender age the type of personality that is going to develop manifests itself in various spontaneous ways. The individual characteristics are present in embryonic form. These will influence the individual's adaptation to the new forces which he finds within himself during the intense growth of adolescence in the physical and emotional fields. A satisfactory adolescence is to a large extent the function of a satisfactory childhood. As the late Fr. King has pointed out:

> "A failure on the part of the conscious personality to cope with newly-emerging elements of sex experience is almost certain to maim the personality and to prevent its harmonious development. . . . Stages in the development of personality, which should have occurred sweetly and naturally during childhood, have to be brought about in the maladjusted adult by laborious and painful efforts, working against half a lifetime of mental and emotional habit and experience."[3]

It is quite possible that personality defects manifested in adolescence and adulthood have their root-cause in inadequate infant training.

[3] *Sex Enlightenment and the Catholic,* L. King, S. J. Bellarmine Series, 10 (1947) pp. 17-18.

Homosexuality has often been considered a problem of adolescence, and the reaction of the adolescent to homosexual experiences will be determined to a large extent by his earlier training. Adolescence is the link between childhood and manhood—continuous with what has gone before and with what will follow. The adolescent must by himself accept his manhood and acknowledge the reality of his male role in adult life. If the adolescent with strong homosexual tendencies has difficulty in adapting himself to the outside world in early life, he may well find that such a difficulty persists in later years.

Homosexuals as a group are notorious for their *feeling of 'not belonging'*, which is generally traceable to the fact that they never really belonged to their parents or their home. Deprived of this natural affection the youth falls more easily into the trap of seduction by an older man who supplants his parents in his affections. For the first time he has become aware of human love but in a homosexual setting. That awareness has brought with it profound emotion—an absorbing happiness to fill a soul so long starved of affection. A new world has revealed itself to him and he has no desire to leave it. In future he invests homosexuality with romantic sentiment which satisfies all his emotional yearnings. The particular friendships of adolescence for such a person may well have such deep emotional significance that they may never be displaced.[4]

---

[4] "Take the case of C. . . . At 15½ years of age, his parents sent him to a holiday camp. . . . He meets a homosexual attendant who fastens on him like a leech on a mastoid. A real, exclusive, jealous, even in a sense enriching love grows up between the two. C is happy, completely happy. He loves and is loved; his adolescent nature is wholly intoxicated. Some

The father of the homosexual may be an alcoholic, cruel to his wife, or he may have shocked the son so gravely in the proceedings that led to divorce, that deep emotional repercussions are felt by the youth. He may blame his father for the loss of his home security and identify himself emotionally with his mother. The same may be said where the mother is the 'guilty partner'. Very often the family background of many practising homosexuals discloses early years spent with a divorced promiscuous parent who encouraged a liberal attitude in the child in matters connected with sex.

Many authorities consider that the ultimate determining factor in homosexuality is due to *faulty sex education*. They attach, for example, a great deal of importance to the way in which elimination training is undertaken. The fact that the parts of the body concerned in these actions are closely concerned with the sex organs may mean that the child will come to associate with the sexual organs the feeling of disgust and shame with which he is taught to

years later, C is still living on these memories. He cannot envisage a heterosexual orientation for his sexuality. He remains true to his first love, like fiancées who, separated by death from their beloved, remain faithful to him with all their heart. Love has been shown to C in its homosexual guise, and he was fully happy. *He does not even think of seeking anything else." New Problems in Medical Ethics*, pp. 83-4.

The case of a 19-year-old follows. "His parents have always been indifferent to him. . . . He has grown up deprived of all affection, alone with himself, imprisoned in the narrow circle of his sorrow and his incompleteness. . . . At the age of 17, B met a companion in the workshop and found sympathy. "For the first time I had the impression of being understood." B asked no more. Used to receiving nothing, it suffices for him that he is understood; he does not even demand to be loved, but he himself loves fervently. . . . Since the birth of that sentiment, B has frequent dreams of sodomic relations between men, and on waking he is assailed with the idea of corporal relations with his friend." *Ibid.*, pp. 77-8.

H

regard his execretory functions.[5] The whole process, which should have been performed as unemotionally as possible, is charged with tension. The child will doubt his capacity to do what is clearly expected of him, so that fear and hostility are aroused towards the demanding mother. For those who accept the Freudian concept of the evolution of sexuality, this is the general explanation given why the erotic zone is mainly transferred from the genitals to the anus as happens in sodomy.[6]

The adolescent's emotional and moral approach to sex is largely conditioned by that of his parents. If for example the adolescent is allowed to regard sex as a simple physical appetite which should be gratified with the same regularity and casualness as hunger and thirst, his sexual behaviour is likely to be very different from that of a boy who has some appreciation of the emotional and spiritual significance of the sex impulse in human beings. The homosexual is marked as one who shows a great lack of understanding of human affective relationships. This must be due in large part to parents who have not extolled self-control and have not shown the sex appetite in its reality as a God-given urge to be used according to His

[5] "We adults must be specially on our guard against the danger of 'projecting' our adult attitude on to juvenile minds and consciences incapable of sustaining such a load. This may quite easily happen not infrequently with grave results when some indecency or similar lapse, which in the mind of the child is in the order of untidiness or disobedience, is visited with a degree of reprobation which would be suitable and justified if the same act had been committed by an adult." *Sex Enlightenment and the Catholic*, p. 13.

[6] "These people will not allow the active partner to touch the genitals and they experience ejaculation only at the climax of anal intercourse." *Society and the Homosexual*, p. 112. But not all those who practise sodomy confine themselves so exclusively to this perversion. The non-Freudian explanation is that anal intercourse is physically the nearest approach to normal intercourse that is possible between men.

laws. Most social workers, too, consider that faulty sex education is their most rewarding field in their search for the causal factors involved in homosexuality.

A recurring factor in the background of many homosexuals is either a *puritanical view of sex* and marital intercourse, or *an attitude of promiscuity* and sexual carelessness, to be *found in the parents*. Puritanism will not reduce the child's sexual urge when he reaches adolescence or adulthood. Since his home training has forbidden him woman, he may well attempt to satisfy himself in homosexual acts.[7] The devil of scrupulosity, which has brought his life to a standstill and surrounded it with taboos, will be cast out later by the Beelzebub of gross, venal sexual practices. If marriage is conceived as a licence to commit lust, the adolescent will strive in his emotional life to separate what he conceives as love from its strong carnal

[7] Le Moal conjures up a case for us. " E has received an upbringing which aimed at being very Christian, but which was in fact Puritanical; instead of developing him, it stifled and repressed him. . . . Initiated only very late to the genital problem . . . he keeps an impression of the disgust which it arouses in him; all *that* is dirty, repugnant, sinful, like the genital organs against which he has been put on his guard. He cannot agree to do so dirty an action. He asks himself how his parents, honourable and pious people, have been able to meet this problem. But the libido is there; woman is forbidden? There remains the man. . . . He conceives of love as sentiment, and he refuses the right of the body to participate in that sentiment. 'To love with the soul only a soul who loves you in the same manner', says André Gide in 'Corydon'. It is the refusal to accept his human reality, his imperfect condition; it is to break the unity of the human composite. When one forbids the body to adopt the same object of love as the heart, and it has all its needs entire, it seeks to satisfy them through homosexuality. . . . Disgust for sexuality, exaggerated respect for female virginity to which one does not dare make an approach; in short, the refusal of the body's right to join with the spirit—such is angelism. The woman is admitted to the heart, but the body has no right to her. And what remains? The man." *New Problems in Medical Ethics*, pp. 84-5.

stamp.[8]  Even were he to marry he would attempt to see his love for his wife as something quasi-mystical.

Sometimes positive steps are taken by the parents to dispel all concepts of objective morality, and the children are initiated at a very early age to all the most intimate details of sexual matters.  Real moral guilt is regarded by the parents as nothing more than a mere deviation from currently accepted social conventions.  Adolescent children of the same sex will be allowed to share the same bed, and sometimes the same room as the parents, where there is a grave danger of their overhearing or possibly seeing parental intercourse.  They may come to imagine coition as something involving physical violence and pain.

The homosexual is often turned away from the world of women because *the too dominant person in his life has been his mother*.  Were one to accept the irreversible state of the five-year-old, then Le Moal's estimate of a proportion of eighty per cent, who owe their homosexuality to their mothers is not surprising, when we remember that up to that time the child is almost completely dependent on his mother.[9]  The homosexual pattern is generally set against the background of a dominant mother and inadequate submissive father,[10] and confessed homosexuals have testified that they denied their male role

[8] "Like the inhabitants of Sodom refusing the daughters of Lot, the homosexual seeks to rejoin the angel whose passage has awakened in him the desire to deny his origin." *Ibid.*, p. 123.

[9] *New Problems in Medical Ethics*, p. 82.

[10] "The father is absent through death, or divorce, or imprisonment, etc.; or he is present, but does not fulfil his role in the home because he is dominated by a too mannish wife.  Secondly, the family being constituted normally or almost normally, then comes the feminine upbringing of the boy": *Ibid.*, p. 81.

because their dominant mother had previously denied them the expression of their masculine characteristics.

The adolescent deprived of all independence by his mother becomes a psychical eunuch, incapable of making a decision. The dominance of the mother is such that she prevents him from reaching emotional maturity by holding him away from the natural father-son relationship. This domination does not provide him with the emotional security necessary for a normal heterosexual life.[11] This over-dependence of the child on the dominant mother is stressed by the British Medical Association's Report as an environmental influence in the causality of homosexuality. Unable to go forward to heterosexuality, he finds an outlet for his sexual urge with those of his own sex. Many, such as Kardiner, see grave danger of the excessive emancipation of women, with the consequent threatening of the patriarchal state of society; they see it as a causative factor in the spread of homosexuality.[12]

[11] "It must be she who arranges his marriage for him; of his own accord he would not think of it. It suffices that he recognizes in himself, with dismay, homosexual tendencies which he has not yet avowed to his mother, though he keeps her informed of his masturbations. . . . He envisages with terror a possible progression on the psychosexual plane. To become heterosexual, to go forward to the conquest of a woman, to found a home, to have children. It is to be obliged to aspire to a better situation, to make this world a reality. He does not feel he has the courage for all this. . . . It is more simple to continue to fight against homosexual tendencies than to embark on that other enterprise." *New Problems in Medical Ethics*, p. 84. Discussing the environmental theory, Odenwald writes: "Homosexuality . . . develops when parents, especially mothers, refuse to assist their children in developing a healthy, independent outlook; when they refuse to untie the apron strings by which they hold and protect their boys; when they do not stimulate their boys to a mature outlook upon life, especially upon sex life; when they 'love' their boys so much that they cannot bear to see them leave the family." *Psychiatry and Catholicism*, p. 387.

[12] The patriarchal state of society is endangered by the over-increasing demands of emancipated women, with a consequent diminishing of male prestige and influence in family affairs, says Kardiner, who stresses the

*Mothers* are sometimes *driven to over-solicitude for their children,* in order to satisfy their own parched emotional feelings. While a mother may sincerely believe she is benefiting her child, and he may appear devoted to her, he develops at the same time a deep hatred and distrust of her because she has robbed him of his manhood.[13] This exploitation of her son's affection to supply her own emotional loss is highlighted when the mother leans too heavily on her son after her husband's death. The mother should not take the child into her bed, to console him or herself, as this practice is difficult to terminate. The child, when asked to leave, may feel he is no longer loved, or, if allowed to stay too long, may develop guilt feelings, so that the concept of going to bed with another woman—his wife—is unimaginable. The

effects that this widespread social change has on the psychology of the individual. After many years of intensive research into the relation between personality types and the structure of society, he concludes that the monogamous, patriarchal family is the most favourable for proper development of the human personality. Kardiner's book, *Sex and Morality* (London, 1955) is an important study of social factors in etiology, especially Chapter VI, ' The Flight from Masculinity '. It is an answer by a sociologist, who is also a practising psychiatrist, to the two Kinsey reports.

[13] Here is the case history of a young man of twenty. He came to the psychoanalyst " because of his great fear of his exclusive concern with men, and complete lack of interest in girls or women. Along with this went increasingly hostile feelings towards his mother. . . . The mother had turned to the boy to satisfy her longing for affection, and . . . she . . . demanded his exclusive devotion. . . . His secret hate and resentment against his mother prevented him from turning to other women as objects of love, since he feared that any affection towards another woman would always carry with it this hidden but intense fear and hatred as well. The love he might have given to another woman could never be withdrawn from his mother in the least degree. . . . The outlook for his future seemed gravely unsatisfactory. . . . Too early and too strong a demand that the boy should take the father's place may thus in the end make it impossible for him ever to feel himself a father or to become so in actuality." This case is given by Susan Isaacs (formerly Head of the Department of Child Development, University of London Institute of Education), *Childhood and After* (London: 1st edition, 1948), pp. 200-1.

mother may treat her husband's memory as so holy or sacrosanct that, even though the child realizes that she is striving to create an unreal picture, he fears he could never attain to such heights. Deprived of his father, who was not only someone to love but also someone to give security and control to his life, he feels unequal to the struggle that such an imitation would involve. On the other hand, the mother may resent her son's showing any feelings for his father and refuse to allow him to mourn. Thus an unreal situation arises, where all feeling must be centred on the mother. Even where there is no outward distress at the loss of his father, it is wise and prudent to assume that such a major happening will affect the child emotionally.

*She loves her son in the wrong way, and makes him a 'mother's boy'.* She demands so much of his time and affections that he has none to give to others, or his love for his mother is so strange that such sharing with other women would be regarded by him as incestuous.[14] Afraid

---

[14] " Since it is universal that every male child, at least at first, is in love with his mother, it naturally follows that a very large proportion of sex development and progress towards heterosexuality is determined by the attitude of the mother." *Their Mothers' Sons*, Edward A. Strecker (Philadelphia, 1946), p. 129.

" When he reaches the age when his mother might well . . . feel a certain jealousy of ' girls ' . . . the invert begins to display . . . signs of inordinate attachment. . . . What has happened? The invert lad, on getting out into the world for the first time, has been rebuffed by both youths and maidens. Try as he may he cannot like girls—on the same terms as boys like them—neither is he ever quite at ease with other boys or they with him. . . . It is only when he finally hears both boys and girls calling him ' Sissy ' that the real tragedy of his condition first appeals him, and that . . . he runs to weep his heart out on his mother's breast. . . . Throughout his life, while drifting farther and farther away from normal intimacy with women, he thrusts himself deeper and deeper into the heart of the only woman he actually really knows—his mother. When he loses her he realizes for the first time that in her he had his only real contact with the lovely things of women, and that on her he had conof losing him, she disapproves of every girl whom he brings home, looking upon them as rivals for her son's affections. She may beseech him to keep away from women as potential carriers of dread diseases, or take him completely into her confidence, revealing to him the failure of her own marriage and the unhappiness involved in such a heterosexual union. If necessary, she may encourage him to engage in homosexual practices, thus fearing less danger of losing him.[15]

There is the *mother who desperately wants a daughter*, and subjects the undesired son to the pattern of her wishful thinking, even to the extent of dressing him in girl's clothes. Communicating her disappointment to him not so much in words as in general attitudes, she will be guilty of his psychical castration. Since he wishes to gain her praise, he will cherish her fond illusion and make up to her by becoming a girl as far as he can. The tragedy is that every child wants to feel that he 'belongs' and that he is loved for himself as he is. Gradually and impercep-

---

centrated all the affection which normal men distribute more . . . generously," *The Invert*, pp. 40-1.

"Such a son, tied and tethered to his mother . . . must find it almost impossible to break away: and to transfer his loyalty to another woman, his wife, must appear as desertion, if not adultery. . . . These men are sons and lovers of their mothers." *The Psychology of Sex*, Oswald Schwarz, (Pelican Books, A194: reprinted 1956), p. 186.

[15] A case in point concerns a practising homosexual of thirty-two years of age, whose father had frequently been away from home during his early childhood. When he confided to his mother that he liked boys like himself she encouraged him, saying, "It is less dangerous to love men than women." When he was analysed he was repeatedly furious with his mother for keeping him to and for herself, thus sanctioning his homosexual practices. "His anger prompted in him the conscious wish to ruin the family reputation and himself. His homosexual affairs became extensive and dangerous to him and his family." 'Etiology and Therapy of Overt Homosexuality', *The Psychoanalytic Quarterly*, Vol. XXIV. No. 4, pp. 506-15. Lawrence Kolb and Adelaide Johnson.

tibly the child assumes a feminine point of view on all things. During adolescence girls instead of boys are his constant companions, and adulthood sees him fixed in his homosexuality. Society has definite views on what constitutes manliness. On account of his inadequate preparation, which should have enabled him to mix with 'masculine' types, he may migrate to the society of other 'mother's boys'. Such homosexuals find employment suited to their talents where there is freedom from conventional restraints, or which afford an opportunity of meeting other homosexuals. This seems the best explanation why certain professions attract such types.

*Sometimes it is the relationship with the father which is at fault.* The father may be so dominated by his wife and so effeminate in his general manner that it is difficult for the son to model his heterosexual orientation on him. On the other hand, the father may be over-athletic and, being the proud possessor of a massive physique himself, demand the same physical prowess from a son constitutionally weaker. The child may thus hate all demonstrations of physical strength and glorifications of manliness. School-teachers in boarding schools are often guilty of this fault in the realms of school sport. This theme was stressed in the stage and screen show 'Tea and Sympathy'. The father of the suspected homosexual advises the schoolmaster to 'make a man' of Tom Lee, his son, the process of which nearly drives the youth to suicide.

Such a sensitive youth will seek excessively his mother's protection and understanding, to the detriment of his emotional progress.   He denies his male role as a protest against manliness.

It is impossible to consider all the different environmental factors which are found recurring in the homosexual's family background, nevertheless those elements already mentioned are the most frequent.   The question arises as to the causal influence which they exercise in the formation of a homosexual bias.   In the foregoing pages of this chapter, we have classified the various types of family backgrounds of known homosexuals.   The main evidence has been provided by confessed homosexuals themselves, who have influenced medical opinion, and they form only a small part of the homosexual world. Any conclusions drawn therefore are confined to the limits of inference.   These homosexual witnesses are generally the victims of some emotional conflict arising from their homosexual practices.[16]   They are unstable characters who are in many cases only too willing to pass on the blame to someone else.

If homosexuality were purely environmental then no explanation would be forthcoming why parents who discover traces of a homosexual bias very early in their child's life are unable to impart to him a more masculine and heterosexual attitude.   In many cases homosexuality is definitely present apparently independently and irrespective of environment.   Many confirmed homosexuals have come from the healthiest heterosexual milieu and many normal heterosexuals are relatively untouched by the most advanced type of the so-called homosexual environment. The environmental theory is based on the assumption

[16] *Homosexuality and Prostitution*, p. 29.

that homosexuals act like women because they have previously thought like them. Yet many homosexuals are
known to act first like women and then afterwards begin
to think like them. There is no disputing the fact that
many cases of homosexuality begin with a desire for
genital satisfaction and since this occurs in a homosexual
setting, the source of genital pleasure is sought again and
again until a bad habit fixation develops.

Finally, background does influence the homosexual
pattern. It is extremely difficult, however, to assess
accurately the extent to which the various elements are
determining factors.[17] Very much depends on the personality and temperament of the particular child. Some
extremists claim fatalistic determination to homosexuality
in every case because of early environmental background.
But we hold that since certain people have a homosexual
tendency of varying intensity, then gravely harmful and
permanent effects may result if these external influences
are brought to bear on it. The reason why some people
evince no homosexual desire despite abnormal features
in their early surroundings is explainable by the fact that
they possess no homosexual potency to be developed, and
thus remain normal. Since it may be stated as a general
principle that a pervading atmosphere of happiness in the
home will lead to a ready acceptance of life in general and
the sex role in particular, it logically follows that a poor
family background will lead to abnormalities. The homosexual tendency in some people is very much fostered by
the factors we have discussed, especially mother domination. Homosexuality is essentially like other sexual
problems, and the influence of these early environmental

[17] *Ibid.*, p. 30.

factors must be estimated accordingly. Case histories show that the emotional structure of some people is so constituted that early environment may in fact determine a more-or-less permanent homosexual approach for the rest of their lives.

# CHAPTER SEVEN

# The Homosexual and his Later
## Social Environment

WE shall now consider the influence of social factors, wider than familial, in order to estimate their importance in the formation of a homosexual condition. These are reduced to *two main categories, segregation and homosexual initiation.*

Normal heterosexual development is impeded by undue and *abnormal segregation in childhood and adolescence.* It is difficult to expect the adult in later life to love a member of the female sex whom he has never been allowed to meet, and who consequently in later life in no way stimulates his affection or imagination. Sexual feelings of adolescents are much stronger than parents and others responsible for their formation care to admit. Many homosexuals blame one-sex boarding schools for their abnormality. They attribute this not so much to their actual homosexual experiences, as to the emotional awareness of other youths fostered by the unbalanced environment in which they were deprived for long periods of female society at this important stage of their emotional lives. While it is true that this is more often than not a rationalization on the part of practising homosexuals, yet it cannot always be dismissed as easily as that. Very often it is at this stage, influenced by earlier factors, that the youth falls in love with another of his own sex, and this is of such intensity that future years will be unable to dispel its memory. He has experienced a deep emotion, and has no desire to seek for another of a different kind.

But in later life, too, segregation may have its evil effects. The last world war, though concluded over a decade ago, has still left its mark on the emotional lives of the soldiers involved in the conflict. This alone affords us ample evidence that sexual segregation affects more or less permanently the sexual lives of adults. In the armed forces[1], prisoner-of-war camps, and other abnormal all-male conditions, men became aware of their homosexual tendencies, perhaps for the first time. There are numerous instances of men who engaged in homosexual practices in these surroundings and were unable or unwilling when normal conditions were restored to assume the heterosexual role. This attitude resulted in the break-up of many marriages.[2] Many men reverted to normal when female company was restored—in fact the majority did so—but the facility and extent of their reorientation was

[1] " From all the evidence available it is, in my opinion, safe to conclude that those problems of sex which may exist in the Services are really problems of certain conditions of life which arise in the Services. . . . The two real dangers are the confirmed homosexual non-commissioned officer who may use the authority of his rank to intimidate young servicemen, and the male prostitute type. The sooner they are recognized as such and discharged from the Service, the better." ' Problem of Sex in the Services.' *The Practitioner*, April 1954, p. 394.

[2] The case of a research scientist who was a prisoner-of-war for four years. " He married before he joined the Services and enjoyed heterosexual relations. . . . Fairly soon after his capture he experienced homosexual stirrings. . . . Eventually he formed an association with another prisoner. . . . He returned to his wife, but continued with his overt homosexuality. Two years ago his wife divorced him." *Society and the Homosexual*, p. 53.

largely dependent on the nature and measure of their homosexual experiences, and the length of their segregation.

The political tension of present-day society, which up till recently in England forced conscription on young men, thus prolonging another two years segregation at the critical age of 18-20, is often blamed for the quasi-inevitable consequences of increased homosexual practices. Society is also to blame for overcrowding in prisons, and reformatories where lack of due supervision has made it an established fact that such places provide favourable opportunities for homosexual practices.[3] There are probably more homosexual acts committed by prisoners than by any other section of the community—according to Fishman as many as 30-40% of the inmates are involved.[4] The depressing outlook, loneliness and boredom of prison-life, the viciousness and low moral standards of the prisoners, the feeling of rejection by society, will all contribute to the prevalence of homosexual practices. 'Solitary vices' are by no means solitary in the intimacy of an over-crowded prison cell where sex often becomes the main preoccupation and subject of conversation; such acts easily become mutual, and develop into more complete homosexual practices. The greater danger is, however, that the friend of the homosexual will be tempted to adopt his *outlook* as well as his

[3] Sir Robert Boothby in the House of Commons Debate on Homosexuality commented, " Our prisons today, in their present overcrowded condition, are factories for the manufacture of homosexuality. . . . It is absolute madness to send these people [homosexuals] to our ordinary overcrowded prisons and put them quite frequently in a cell with others and even in a dormitory together." *They Stand Apart*, p. 208.

[4] Fishman was the Chief Inspector of Federal Prisons in the United States. His findings are published in his book, *Sex in Prison* (New York, 1934).

sexual habits. He will be accepted into the close-knit secret society of the prison underworld—a preparation for his future secretive life as a confirmed practising homosexual.

Homosexual acts in these all-male surroundings must not be considered in isolation, but connected with the emotional approach of the individual concerned. These homosexual acts may only prove that the present available male is chosen as a poor substitute for the unavailable but still desirable female.[5] Far graver than the conditioning of the body by repeated acts, is that of the emotions in all-male surroundings. The friend of the homosexual will be drawn into a relationship so deep that it could be described as 'love'. A chance homosexual act rarely makes a man into a homosexual for the rest of his life, but what often happens is that in these all-male surroundings an intense emotional attachment is established which dominates his future life. Therefore *the emotional danger of segregation must be stressed* rather than the physical expression of homosexual acts as a causative factor of homosexuality.

What part does *homosexual initiation* play in fixing the homosexual condition? The records of psychiatrists show that over ninety per cent of homosexual cases start by seduction.[6] These homosexual acts are regarded by Freud as merely the final stage of what is an inevitable result of 'sex'. Man, the victim of his sexual drive and urge, must eventually express himself sexually at some

[5] 'Anomaly' comments as regards prisoners: "on their return to everyday society the normal men remained normal, remembering these prison affairs only as strong and perverted interludes: while the inverts remained inverted as ever." *The Invert*, p. 212.

[6] *Society and the Homosexual*, p. 64.

time of his life. If his inborn condition is homosexual, then his sexual acts will be homosexual in character. The only alternative is to struggle against these tendencies using repression or sublimation aided perhaps by religious ideals. The result however is nearly always the same— psychic eruption or some gross, excessive, sexual perversions by which he releases the pent-up sexual urges. In fact the ones most likely to find themselves in trouble with the law, says Westwood, are "the pious men, the strong-minded men, the men who have established themselves in the community."[7]

Sex-initiation is therefore the passing-into-act and consciousness of an already pre-existing, subconscious, inborn condition. Sexual acts, of whatever nature, cannot alter a man's basic sexual condition. Homosexual acts, in such a theory, are the occasion and not the cause of homosexuality. The only possible importance that would be attached to these homosexual practices is the strengthening of existing tendencies if these acts are of frequent occurrence.

Opposed to this view are those who hold that homosexual initiation is the cause and occasion of homosexuality. Homosexuality is looked upon as a proselytizing religion. In 'They Stand Apart' Viscount Hailsham claims that there is no single factor except direct initiation which can account for the phenomenal increase since 1938.

"The problem of male homosexuality is in essence the problem of corruption of youth by itself and by its elders. It is the problem of the creation by means of such corruption of new addicts ready to corrupt a still further generation of young men and boys in the future."[8]

[7] *Ibid.*, p. 44.        [8] *They Stand Apart*, p. 29.

I

If this is true then the temporary nature of homosexual unions will cause a constant urge and desire in the homosexuals to seek out new blood. The British Medical Report emphasises the fact that

"homosexual practices tend to spread by contact, and from time to time they insidiously invade certain groups of the community which would otherwise be predominantly heterosexual".[9]

What is the correct solution? What importance should be attached to homosexual experiences as a determinant of the homosexual condition? There are many homosexuals whose background indicates no apparent abnormal physical or psychological features, and whose homosexual bias began by seeking sexual gratification at the homosexual level.[10] It is incorrect to state categorically that the reason they sought this type of sexual activity is due to hidden factors unknown to medicine and psychiatry, inevitably determining the person to this manner of sexual expression. This is to place the homosexual propensity outside the realms of bad-habit formation, which is the point in question. For the purpose of accuracy we shall consider the importance that should be attributed to homosexual initiation under three sets of circumstances:

[9] *Homosexuality and Prostitution*, p. 16.
[10] "Sometimes, however, this process which begins with a mood of affection and degenerates into carnal passion is reversed, and we see homosexuality beginning by a purely genital satisfaction. The initiation has been made by an older companion or by an adult. The pleasure then felt is in some sort a discovery of a world until then unknown and which is sought again. Little by little the erogenous sphere is extended; from the simple, fleeting adventures in one certain place, the subject passes on to long acts of tenderness. His emotions participate in it, and his mind runs the risk of adhering to this parody of love and of going astray in it." *New Problems in Medical Ethics*, p. 111.

(a) *where both parties are adolescents; (b) where one party is an adult and the other an adolescent; (c) where both parties are adults.*

Many sexologists and psychologists see in particular *exclusive friendships of adolescents* a phase of homosexuality just because the partners happen to be of the same sex.[11] This is nothing more than to tie on a convenient tag to explain adolescent behaviour without exploring the psychological background. It may just be curiosity, however unhealthy, seeking to satisfy itself.

Again it may be merely adolescent sexual passion expressing itself in the only available means possible due to circumstances and conditions of life, such as a boys' boarding school. There is no doubt that during this period of adolescence, healthy, valuable, virtuous and enriching friendships spring up between boys. Even though the dangers of such a situation are obvious, it is a great mistake to jump to the worst conclusions in every case in which signs of such an attachment are observed. Such friendships are of inestimable value to the persons concerned.

Even in those cases where the school records show that the now adult homosexual engaged in homosexual practices as a youth, one is not thereby always justified in concluding that such adolescent homosexual practices were the sole cause of his abnormality.[12] This would

[11] " We have a strongly sensual description of such friendships in Roger Peyrefitte's book: *Les Amitiés Particulières*. ' I love you more than my life ', says one of the adolescents to the other. And that we may understand the meaning of the embraces of two college boys, the author adds, somewhat heavily; ' Did he still believe, that young boy, that he spoke only the language of friendship? ' " *Ibid.*, pp. 110-1.

[12] " When one investigates the school history of invert men it is found that most of them were not infamous for youthful indiscretions of a homosexual nature." *The Invert*, p. 143.

seem tantamount to saying that the sole cause of a normal youth's heterosexuality is to be found in his normal sexual acts with a girl.  On the contrary many who were known at school to have engaged in homosexual practices developed into perfectly normal men.  Since the effects of homosexual acts vary with the individual—dependent on character, standards of morality, strength of homosexual tendencies, etc.—it will often be found that many youths who are thought at first to be homosexual are later discovered to be normal.  This normality may show itself when they are brought in contact with those of the opposite sex.  Therefore it must be said that adolescent homosexual behaviour is not an inevitable accompaniment or evident sign of homosexuality.

"Nevertheless," says Larère, "thanks to the study of a certain number of cases, one definite point seems well established, namely, that homosexuality often begins at that age, in a first psychological shock accompanied by a strong surge of emotion.  With the adolescent, preferential love for a partner of the same sex will sometimes fix the strength of his libido and will arrest the normal development of instinct."[13]

Sexual difficulties at adolescence have an important bearing on our problem.  Sex means more to the adolescent than a question of mere mechanics.  It becomes something close-up, charged with emotion and highly personal.  He visualizes it as something unique, and tends to lose sight of the fact that others have passed through successfully, and others are passing, or will pass through the same phase.  The period of adolescence will vary with

[13] *New Problems in Medical Ethics*, p. 110.

the individual from practically overnight to several years, and in that period he feels alone in his enigma.

*Masturbation* with its trials is often the cause of exaggerated feelings of inferiority and irrational guilt complexes, and unless properly handled may end in serious neurotic disturbances. There are very different psychological reactions to masturbatory practices in introvert and extrovert personalities. The extrovert may practise masturbation without any apparent internal stress or grave pangs of conscience, whereas the sensitive introvert with high ideals of purity may find these ideals shattered from time to time. Chronic masturbation may well arrest the normal sexual development. It may be a symptom of a narcissistic homoerotic disposition. When the turmoil of puberty has subsided and the psycho-sexual attraction settles finally on the opposite sex, the adolescent who has not learned to control his masturbatory habits may well remain fixed in phantasms of the same sex. Except in cases of seduction in extreme youth, it is extremely rare to find a homosexual who has not at some time during adolescence contracted a habit of masturbation. In conditions of segregation especially, the narcissistic preoccupation with his own genitals leads to an awakened interest in other male genitals rather than in speculation or phantasy on the female organs. It is in this way that masturbation can lead to homosexual acts in boyhood. There is no doubting that segregation in school during this period of sexual activity is in many cases the reason for homosexual fixation as the adolescent's only world is peopled with those of his own sex. This emotional fixation, linked with homosexual practices, often leads to the formation of a compulsive habit.

What is true of other sexual difficulties at adolescence is also true where homosexual acts are concerned. The significance of adolescent homosexual acts is often grossly exaggerated, however, and the consequences are not always as disastrous as is at first feared. Yet sex variant activity is harmful to a normal sexual life. The more one indulges in these abnormal practices the more difficult is a heterosexual orientation in later life. Seduction or sex initiation, for example, may alter the mental attitude of the seduced so that his future sexual phantasies are of a homosexual nature which will eventually exclude the heterosexual attraction. If the constitutional nature of homosexuality were satisfactorily proved, then even in this theory homosexual acts bring a latent condition to consciousness and the sexual appetite is aroused. The existing tendencies will also be strengthened, thus rendering heterosexuality more difficult to attain.

Schoolboy friendships for those with strong homosexual tendencies often become real 'love affairs', and indecent acts, if present, are far more significant for them than for normal youths. Such acts mark their actual sexual awakening and are mile-stones in their psycho-sexual life. These acts constitute the main determinant of their homosexual fixation.

Is there any practical criterion which one could use to distinguish the homosexual from the normal youth? One guiding rule is that where the circumstances are unfavourable for homosexual practices and the youth deliberately seeks to create such circumstances which would afford him the opportunity of gratifying his homosexual desires, then it is probable that such an adolescent has a more or less strong homosexual bias. This differs very much from the normal youth who performs homosexual acts, perhaps out of curiosity, in an environment favourable at the moment.

In close friendships between older and younger boys it may happen that there is a profound hero-worship on the part of the younger, with no affectionate reciprocation on the part of the elder. When the younger boy is fundamentally normal he may be only satisfying his curiosity, and the affair has not much significance for him. It may well be discovered also that the older boy's phantasy is homosexual but such a state of affairs cannot always be taken for granted. In certain cases, particularly where the affection is not accompanied by sexual acts, a boy of fifteen to seventeen may 'fall in love romantically' at a segregated school with an attractive pre-pubescent boy simply because the latter, with smooth skin, treble voice and so on, is not yet in the physical sphere fully masculine. Mentally, too, the aggressive dominant male characteristics are not yet fully developed. In such cases the elder boy is not necessarily homosexual, but will turn in course of time quite naturally from the girl-substitute to the real woman.

In cases of homosexual acts at schools it is inevitable that the older boy, as presumably the more responsible, receives most of the blame and punishment. Nevertheless it is important to bear in mind that the older boy is not in all cases the seducer.

Some authorities, then, see the youth as a substitute for the woman so that the homosexual is physically attracted by the likeness of the adolescent to the female body. However the common type of homosexuality is essentially between two adults. Infanto-homosexual practices involve a much more complicated abnormality.[14]   In fact many homosexuals see no attraction in the adolescent precisely because he is so feminine.[15]   It is wrong therefore to read homosexual meanings into the most innocent *associations between adults and adolescents*.   If homosexual acts do take place, the conclusion to be drawn seems to be the presence of some psychopathic disorder in the adult rather than any sexual predilection for the adolescent.

The adult homosexual may approach the youth for very simple, practical reasons—less danger of blackmail and exposure with more hope of success in his attempts at sexual satisfaction.   The paederast constitutes a different problem from that of the homosexual, as he is often of the same age-mentality as the youth whom he introduces to homosexual practices.   Confessed adult homosexuals in England who clamour for a repeal of the law punishing consenting adults committing overt homosexual acts in private are practically unanimous in their condemnation

---

[14] " The infanto-homosexuals are attracted to young boys.   It is a much more complicated perversion, because not only is the sexual impulse directed to the same sex, but also the normal associations of a sexual attraction are sacrificed.   In spite of popular ideas to the contrary it is rare to find a man who is greatly attracted to both men and boys.   Male homosexuality may run the whole gamut from ardent sensuality to spiritual love, but it is essentially between two men who know what they are doing and who, in spite of all the pressures of society, find that they can only be sexually stimulated by members of their own sex."  *Society and the Homosexual*, pp. 24-5.

Dr. Neustatter concludes from case histories that seducers of young persons are " often . . . frankly psychopathic . . . and . . . have a complete inability to appreciate that there is anything morally wrong in their acts."  *They Stand Apart*, pp. 108-9.

[15] " The invert is usually attracted by those who are definitely of male appearance, probably mature, and often rough.   Thus [the homosexual] is especially troubled by a susceptibility to those who are most likely to resent his affection."  *The Invert*, p. 71.

of the infanto-homosexual.[16] Yet seduction by a dissolute homosexual is by far the most dangerous type of homosexual initiation. One must be careful however to establish who is actually the seducer, as the youth in a minority of cases may be responsible for the overtures.[17]

Schools, scout and youth movements do attract many well-meaning unconscious homosexuals[18] who consider their vocation from very lofty motives, but it also acts as a magnet to other less well-intentioned homosexuals. Court cases in England recently brought to light the startling fact that many immoral teachers, already convicted of homosexual offences with their pupils, have secured another teaching post on their release from prison without any apparent difficulty. What often happens if a court case is involved is that the cross-questioning drives the facts deeper into the impressionable mind of the adolescent thereby arousing a curiosity which may have been absent before. The observance of a strict judicial pro-

[16] " There are some homosexuals who do not feel any guilt on account of their homosexuality, nor do they feel that they are doing wrong in carrying on homosexual practices with consenting adults, though they would feel that it was extremely wrong to commit them with children or adolescents." *Homosexuality and Prostitution*, p. 46.

[17] The case of the schoolmaster who had been in charge of a dormitory of boys. " One of the boys whose previous innocence was open to doubt, used to come and sit on his bed and fool about. This was too great a temptation, and finally the schoolmaster, an otherwise upright man with a good war record, succumbed, and sexual incidents went on for a year until he was caught." *They Stand Apart*, p. 136.

[18] " One can hardly fail to be struck by the considerable number of young men who come to education urged thereto by morbid instincts. The danger is not so much in the existence of the deviation, against which it is often possible to react, as in the victim's ignorance of it and, consequently, in its strengthening by reason of a propitious atmosphere. Where the young teacher, in all good faith, believes that he has discovered in himself a vocation for teaching, there is nothing more than a hunger for danger, like the moth which finds itself attracted by the flames only to have its wings burned." *New Problems in Medical Ethics*, p. 73.

cedure in such cases is often more damaging than the actual seduction itself.[19]

Among the least dangerous of all forms of homosexual initiations are *homosexual acts between adults*, since the adult is better equipped than the adolescent to deal with the emotional influences aroused by sexual expression. All homosexual acts are dangerous in so far as they give rise to habit formation as well as strengthening existing tendencies, but there is less danger of the adult's emotions going astray.

The effects of homosexual initiation vary with circumstances, but it has its most demoralizing result where the adolescent is seduced by a dissolute adult. This seduction, in common with others, will have less far-reaching consequences where the youth comes from a good home and has a sound training in character formation. As the British Medical Association's Report says;

"A healthy social environment, springing from secure and happy homes which give a sound background of character training, and where sex is kept in its rightful place, would be the greatest prophylactic. Boys and girls from homes where high moral standards are aimed at, where there is parental harmony, sensible, but not over-strict, discipline, a

[19] "The effect of Court proceedings on juveniles involved in cases of homosexual offences is unsatisfactory. The mental stress caused in a child by the inquisition in a court of law may be much more harmful to him than the seduction itself. Permanent harm may be caused to a minor when he has to repeat his evidence in one court after another. If a case is adjourned from a lower to a higher court—weeks or months may elapse between the hearings and throughout the period child witnesses have to keep in their minds the sordid incident and all its objectionable details. The Committee recommends that in a magistrate's court proceedings which involve child witnesses should be as informal as possible." *Homosexuality and Prostitution*, p. 36.

general recognition of personal responsibility and sincere religious faith, will not easily fall a prey to the seducer's invitations to homosexual or heterosexual misconduct."[20]

Yet homosexual experience in adolescence is often the determining factor of a permanent homosexuality especially where it is allied to strong homosexual tendencies, poor family background and is highly charged with emotional values.

Conditioned reflexes play an important part in all habit-formations, and there can be hardly any doubt that the form in which the sexual instinct expresses itself is largely determined by experiences in which it was first aroused and first dealt with. There are many practising homosexuals who owe their deviation to a repetition of overt homosexual acts begun in adolescence.[21] Their homosexual component whether strong or weak will have been further strengthened by repeated acts until the heterosexual bias was 'laid over' by a homosexual propensity.

Where the homosexual tendencies have expressed themselves in act, then a cure, in so far as a heterosexual reorientation is attempted, is rendered far more difficult.[22]

[20] *Homosexuality and Prostitution*, p. 41.

[21] "Homosexual tendencies are, at some time or another, present in almost every normal individual, and, during adolescence, they are often the prevalent emotional tendency. What makes an active homosexual out of an otherwise normal individual is the predominance and fixation of this tendency in adult life, coupled with the acquisition of the habit of securing satisfaction of it by physical homosexual practices." *They Stand Apart*, pp. 21-2.

[22] "If, however, homosexuality is something which is acquired from environment by the fixation in a false predominance of a tendency almost always existing in normal individuals, it is unfortunately also true that, once permanently fixed by an established routine of sexual satisfaction, a homosexual can never be 'cured' in the sense of making him invulnerable to temptation by members of his own sex. This, at least, appears to be true in the present state of medical science." *Ibid.*, p. 22.

Yet there are many chaste homosexuals who do not, and cannot, owe their sexual deviation to homosexual practices. Nevertheless, *acquired homosexuality by initiation and indulgence must be admitted as the main causative factor in a large number of homosexual cases.* The major influencing role, however must be attributed to the emotions which accompany such homosexual acts.

# CHAPTER EIGHT

## *Objective Morality*

CHRISTIAN tradition and Biblical sources condemn as sinful homosexual practices which they regard always as involving wilful evil-doing. In recent times it is urged that these sources took little account of the homosexual condition, their whole orientation being directed towards the condemnation of homosexual acts. These acts were considered an abomination and were an example of what St. Paul calls the "reprobate mind"—the deliberate refusal to acknowledge God's laws, though they are manifestly declared in His works for all to understand.[1] On this point Dr. Bailey writes:

> "It is clear that the Bible condemns as sinful the practices of those whom we may call homosexual perverts. But does it also brand as sinful the acts to which a genuine invert may be impelled, not by moral obliquity, but by a disorder of the sexual nature for which he (or she) cannot be held responsible? We can only say that this is a question to which neither Testament affords an answer, since inversion and its peculiar problems were unknown to antiquity. . . . Today, however, the situation is different, and the sexual behaviour of the invert gives rise to problems which call for special consideration—though we must be careful not to misinterpret the silence of Scriptures on this matter."[2]

[1] Rom. i. 28.

[2] *Sexual Offenders and Social Punishment*, pp. 70-1. In the chapter we have followed the same sources mentioned by Dr. Bailey in his book, *Homosexuality and the Western Christian Tradition*.

Our main concern is with the moral responsibility of homosexuality, whether of condition or practices, in the light
of recent medical and psychiatric evidence.   We shall
sketch briefly, however, the main features that have determined the Christian condemnation of homosexual practices, and implicitly of the homosexual condition itself.

Consideration of the Christian attitude to homosexual
practices begins with the story of the destruction of Sodom
and Gomorrah, and this event has exercised a powerful
influence upon the evolution of the ecclesiastical and civil
attitudes to homosexuality.   It is cited as authoritative
in legislation from the *novellae* of Justinian (538) to the
canons of the third Lateran Council (1179), and it has
traditionally been taken for granted that the sin for which
the cities were destroyed was that of their addiction to
homosexual practices.

What is the meaning of the incident recorded in Gen.
xix. 4-11?   Did that incident constitute only one proof
among many of the wickedness of the people of Sodom?
Were they so notoriously addicted to homosexual practices that this vice alone was the cause of the divine
destruction of the city?   A brief account of the circumstances which led up to the events described in Gen. xix,
is the obvious starting-point of any investigation.   When
Lot parted from Abraham he decided to settle in Sodom,
a city so exceedingly wicked that its sins cried to Heaven
for vengeance.   Abraham interceded with God not to
destroy the city if he could but find ten just men among
its inhabitants.

One must study the preceding chapter in order to
understand both the Angels' purpose in going to Sodom,
and God's clear intention to destroy the city because of

its wickedness. God decided to ascertain for Himself the true state of affairs as regards the morals of the city, and accordingly sent two angels to investigate. These divine messengers were given hospitality by Lot, but before they retired for the evening, the house was besieged by the male inhabitants who demanded that the visitors be brought out so that the Sodomites might 'know' them. Lot attempts to dissuade them from their evil purpose, and offers to produce his daughters, whom the Sodomites might abuse at will on condition that they do not 'do' anything against Lot's distinguished visitors. The crowd persist however in their original demand and are ultimately thwarted by the angels. When Lot and his family with their visitors had left the city the following morning it was destroyed by fire and brimstone from Heaven.

Examining the text itself, we find the traditional conception of the homosexual sin of Sodom is based on verse 5: "Bring them (Lot's visitors) out hither that we may know them." The word here translated 'know' comes from the Hebrew *yādha'* which can mean 'engage in coition' and the question revolves round whether or not it has a sexual signification here. Dr. Bailey presented, as his personal contribution to the Wolfenden Committee in their investigations of the homosexual problem, his book *Homosexuality and the Western Christian Tradition*. He suggests that *yādha'* merely means 'seeking information' and thus the Sodomites are represented as desiring to check the bona fides of Lot's guests as their host may have exceeded his rights as a '*gēr*' or sojourner in the city. This is the explanation given why the Sodomites beset Lot's house in force. Dr. Bailey bases his argument on the fact that if homosexual practices were implied then the word used should have been *shākhabh* which means 'lie' in the coital sense, as this is the most commonly used word in the Old Testament to describe homosexual, heterosexual and bestial intercourse.

*Shākhabh* is a clear and unmistakable term and could have been used by the author if all the inhabitants desired was to 'lie' with the visitors. *Shākhabh*, however, implies sinful intercourse to which both parties consent and is obviously unsuited to the present incident where the intention of the Sodomites was to abuse or rape Lot's guests. The guests were angels and could not sin. While we admit that *yādha'* can signify something other than 'coition', yet in the Old Testament it is used eleven times, excluding the present text, expressly for that purpose.[3] Six references occur in Genesis, and in a further five places it is used in conjunction with *mishkābh* to denote the act of lying.[4]

What is the meaning of *yādha'* in Gen. xix. 4? In another parallel story which is found in Judges xix, the word *yādha'* is used to signify 'homosexual abuse': "Bring forth the man that came into thy house that we may abuse (*yādha'*) him." It should also be noted that in verse 8 of the same chapter in Genesis, when in reply to the Sodomites' demand that the visitors be produced so that they might 'know them', Lot replies that he has two daughters who as yet have not known (*yādha*) men. The *Bible de Jerusalem* interprets the present verses in an explicitly homosexual sense: "amene-les-nous pour que

[3] Gen. iv. 1, 17, 25; xix. 8; xxiv. 16; xxxviii. 26.   Judg. xi. 39; xix. 22, 25. I Sam. i. 19.   I Kings i. 4.
[4] Num. xxxi. 17, 18, 35.   Judg. xxi. 11, 12.

nous en abusions".[5] *La Sainte Bible* also gives *yādha'* a specifically sexual signification in the present context "Ils intimèrent alors à Lot de faire sortir ces hommes qui étaient entres chez lui pour les 'connaître', selon l'euphémisme employé par la Bible pour esprimer les rapports charnels".[6]  Both these sources describe the intentions of the Sodomites as a desire to commit homosexual acts against the visitors to their city.[7]

The interpretation of the story of Sodom's destruction does not rest on one word, but on the whole context. Sodom was a wicked city which God intended to destroy if ten just men were not found by the angels.  "What is recorded as having happened is clear enough," says *The Interpreter's Bible* (a non-Catholic source).  "The men of the city demanded that Lot hand over his guests to them that they gratify their unnatural lust.  He tried to resist the extreme outrage which the lustful gang in Sodom were about to perpetrate upon the men who had harborage in his house."[8]

Dr. Bailey's argument as to the desire of the Sodomites to check the bona fides of the visitors could in no way account for the shattering events recorded in Genesis. Lot pleads with the Sodomites after their demand to 'know' his visitors: "Do not so, I beseech you, my brethren, do not commit this evil."[9]  The situation is so dangerous that Lot has recourse to desperate measures—

[5] *Bible de Jerusalem*—Paris (1953), p. 94.
[6] *Le Sainte Bible*—Paris (1953), p. 291.
[7] 'Le vice contre nature—Et le pire est que le désir de ces garçons libertins et de ces vieillards impurs s'excitait sur des Anges de Dieu.' *Bible de Jerusalem*, p. 94.  'Le vice contre nature dont le nom dérive de celui de la ville de Sodome était très répandu dans l'antiquité. *La Sainte Bible*, p. 291.
[8] *The Interpreter's Bible*—New York (1952) p. 627.
[9] Gen., xix. 7.

K

his daughters are offered by him to the lustful citizens:
"abuse you them as it shall please you so that you do no
evil to these men"[10]   The citizens persist in their
demands and still try to enter Lot's house but are unable
to do so: "And them (the citizens) they (the angels)
struck with blindness from the least to the greatest, so that they could not find the door."[11]   The
visitors tell Lot to prepare to leave the city, for they
intend to destroy the place "because their cry is grown
loud before the Lord, who hath sent us to destroy
them".[12]

In the face of such overwhelming evidence of their evil
ways, God's threatened vengeance cannot be withheld any
longer.   That *all* the Sodomites were guilty that night
of desiring to perform homosexual acts with Lot's visitors
is obvious from the Hebrew word *miqqâseh*.   In verse 4
this word signifies literally 'from the extremity', and in
the context should read 'from every corner (of the city)'.
*La Sainte Bible* commenting on this verse, says that all,
both young and old, came to satisfy their passion, showing only too well the perversity of the city where not even
ten just men could be found.[13]   The word *miqqâseh*, it
holds, should be interpreted in the sense of 'all' or 'to
the last men'".[14]   The same word *miqqâseh* in Gen. xlvii.
2, signifies that no one is excluded: "Five men also the

[10] Gen. xix. 8.
[11] Gen. xix. 11.
[12] Gen. xix. 13.
[13] *La Sainte Bible*, p. 291.
[14] 'Informés rapidement de la présence des hôtes de Lot, viennent tous,
jeunes et vieux, pour assouvir leur passion, ne montrant ainsi que trop la
perversité de la cité ou l'on aurait même pas trouvé dix justes'. . . .
L'expression miqqâseh " depuis l'extremité, la fin " rendue dans les versions
" ensemble " doit s'entendre dans la sens de tous, jusqu'au dernier.' *Ibid.*,
p. 291.

last (*miqqâseh*) of his brethren, he presented before the king." It is pointless now for the angels to continue their search for ten just Sodomites since all the citizens were involved in the outrage. The visitors' task is completed, and since the *condicio sine qua non* of the city's survival is not fulfilled, it must be destroyed.

From this brief examination of text and context we may conclude that *yādha' has a sexual meaning in the text, indeed a homosexual one*, and this is confirmed by the context. The Sodomites intended to commit homosexual acts and their proposed victims were Lot's visitors. We cannot exclude the possibility that other evil practices contributed causally to the destruction of the city, but the homosexual desires manifested that evening were the proximate cause, at least partial, of subsequent events. All the Sodomites were guilty of intending to commit homosexual acts, and this furnished the necessary proof of the sinfulness of the city—no just men could be found. However, there is no means of establishing from the Scripture the actual extent of homosexual practices among the Sodomites.

It is obvious from the context of the Sodom Story that the destruction of Sodom and Gomorrah was a divinely-sent punishment, and their sudden complete devastation created an indelible impression upon future generations. "The two cities are mentioned as cities of appalling wickedness," says *The Interpreter's Bible*, "with the implication that those who imitate them will meet the same fate."[15]

That this has been the constant Christian Tradition of the Sodom story is shown clearly by *Biblical and Patristic*

[15] *Op cit.*, p. 630.

*sources which condemn Sodom's wickedness.* The Old
Testament depicts Sodom as a symbol of utter destruction[16] and its sins as being of such magnitude and scandal
as to merit exemplary punishment:

"And the men of Sodom were very wicked and sinners
before the face of the Lord, beyond measure." Gen. xiii. 13.

"And the Lord said: The cry of Sodom is multiplied, and
their sin is become exceedingly grievous." Gen. xviii. 20.

"And I have seen the likeness of adulterers and the way of
lying in the prophets of Jerusalem: . . . They are all
become to me as Sodom and the inhabitants thereof as
Gomorrah." Jer. xxiii. 14.

"Behold this was the iniquity of Sodom. . . . They were
lifted up and committed abominations before me and I took
them away as thou hast seen." Ez. xvi. 49-50.

The same theme, as to the cause of the cities' destruc-
tion (namely their evil ways), is found recurring in the
New Testament.  In Jude 7, we find that the sin of
Sodom is identified as being of a homosexual nature.

"And whosoever shall not receive you nor hear your words,
going forth out of that house or city shake off the dust from
your feet.  Amen I say to you, it shall be more tolerable
for the land of Sodom and Gomorrah in the day of judgement than for that city." Matthew x. 14-15.[17]

"And reducing the cities of the Sodomites and of the
Gomorrhites into ashes, condemned them to be overthrown,
making them an example to those that should after act
wickedly." II Peter ii. 6.

[16] Isa. i. 9; xiii. 19; Jer. xlix. 18; Amos iv. 11; Soph. ii. 9.
[17] The same idea recurs in Matt. xi. 23-24; and in Luke x. 12.

" As Sodom and Gomorrah and the neighbouring cities, in like manner, having given themselves to fornication, and going after *other flesh*, were made an example, suffering the punishment of eternal fire." Jude 7.

"Other flesh" in the last quotation is thus explained by Estius. "*Caro altera intelligit carnem masculam*," firstly because "*caro altera*" is understood to signify "*caro aliena*", and secondly because "*caro mascula respectu masculae semper manet caro aliena*".[18] Nevertheless, apart from this one explicit reference, it is difficult to conclude from Scripture alone that Sodom was destroyed solely because of its addiction to homosexual practices. Accordingly we must turn to the testimony of the Fathers and examine their interpretation of the Sodom Story in relation to homosexual practices.

*The Fathers* entertained no doubt whatever that the Sodomites were peculiarly and inordinately addicted to homosexual practices, especially paederasty, and were punished on this account. Four representative passages will suffice to indicate the general view during the Patristic period.

*Clement of Alexandria* (Paed. iii. 8) says that the Sodomites had through much luxury fallen into uncleanness, practising adultery shamelessly, and burning with insane love for boys.[19]

*John Chrysostom* (ad pop. Antioch. hom. xix) says:

". . . the very nature of the punishment was a pattern of the nature of the sin. Even as [the Sodomites] devised a barren coitus, not having for its end the procreation of

[18] Estii, *Pauli Epistolae* VII (Paris, 1844) p. 357.
[19] Migne, PG. 8, 615.

children, so did God bring on them such a punishment as made the womb of the land for ever barren and destitute of all fruits."[20]

The disaster that overtook the cities is regarded by *St. Augustine* as an illustration of cause and effect in the moral sphere. He explains the presence of homosexual acts as being in itself a recompense for other sins, since these acts are not only sins *per sè*, but also the penalties for sins.[21] Augustine writes elsewhere (De civ. Dei xvi. 30) of Sodom, ". . . the impious city, where custom has made sodomy as prevalent as laws have elsewhere made other kinds of wickedness".[22]

Finally there is the *Apostolic Constitution* vii. 2: "Thou shalt not corrupt boys: for this wickedness is contrary to nature and arose from Sodom".[23]

From an examination of the text, context, as well as Biblical and Patristic references to Sodom and Gomorrah, it is evident that the destruction of these cities was due to the wickedness of their inhabitants who, among other vices, were addicted to homosexual practices. Yet quite apart from the texts referring to the events of Sodom and and Gomorrah, there are *other definite Biblical and Pat-*

[20] PG. 49. 191.  Elsewhere in John Chrysostom's works there are references to the sin of Sodom:

Heli. et vid. iv. PG. 51. 340-1.
De perf. carit. vii. PG. 56. 288-9.
In Matt. hom. xlii. 3. PG. 57. 449.
In epist. ad Rom. iv. PG. 60. 415-22.
In epist. I ad Thess. viii. 3. PG. 62. 442-4.
In epist. ad Tit. hom. v. 4. PG. 62. 693.
[21] De nat. et grat. xxii. PL. 44. 258-9.
[22] PL. 41, 509.  Also cf. de mend. vii. 10 PL. 40. 495-6.
Contra mend. ix. 20. 22.  PL. 40. 530-1.
          xvii. 34. PL. 40. 541-3.
          conf. iii. 8. PL. 32. 689-90.
[23] PG. 1. 999.  Also in Const. Apost. vi. 27-28.  PG. I. 979-86.

*ristic references to homosexual practices.* Two passages
are found in the "Holiness Code" of Leviticus.

"Though shalt not lie with mankind, as with womankind;
because it is an abomination (*tō'ēbhāh*)". xviii. 22. Also "If
anyone lie with a man as with a woman, both have committed an abomination (*tō'ēbhāh*): let them be put to
death." xx. 13.

The fact that these laws occur in chapters which
expressly associate homosexual and other immoralities
with the customs of the Chanaanites and Egyptians, seems
to suggest that the object of this legislation was rather to
prevent the contamination of God's people by the evil
ways of their neighbours, than to condemn already existing vices among the Jewish people. This also presupposes
that the nations which surrounded Israel were so addicted
to these immoral practices as to endanger the morals of
the Hebrews. There is always a tendency to exaggerate
the vices of one's enemies, and the conflicting views of
historians do not allow us to make a definite judgement in
this matter. This does not alter the fact that the Biblical
texts from Leviticus condemn homosexual practices in
themselves in the strongest terms.

The attitude of the Hebrews to homosexual practices,
as reflected in the Old Testament, was certainly not one
of approval or toleration. In common with other
major crimes it was punishable by death—though there
is no evidence that the supreme penalty was ever inflicted.
The word *tō'ēbhāh*, while closely associated with idolatry,
denotes also the conduct of those who serve false gods,
and it is often extended to signify whatever reverses the
proper order of things, such as homosexual practices.

This seems to be the connection in Leviticus, since homosexual acts exemplify the spirit of idolatry and are subversions of the true order.

Focusing our attention on the New Testament we find three passages which refer to homosexual practices:

" And in like manner, the men also, leaving the natural use of the women, have burned in their lusts, one towards another: men with men, working that which is filthy and receiving in themselves the recompense which was due to their error." Rom. i. 27.

"Know you not that the unjust shall not possess the kingdom of God?  Do not err: neither fornicators, nor idolators nor adulterers: nor the effeminate (*malakoi*—Vulg. *molles*) nor liers with mankind (*arsenokoitai*—Vulg., *masculorum concubitores*), nor thieves nor covetous nor drunkards nor railers nor extortioners shall possess the kingdom of God." I Cor. vi. 9-10.

"Knowing this: that the law is not made for the just but for the unjust . . . for them who defile themselves with mankind (*arsenokoitai*—Vulg. *Masculorum concubitores*)." I Tim. i. 9-10.

St. Paul in the Epistle to the Romans expressly denounces both male and female homosexual practices as contrary to nature and characteristic of the "reprobate mind" of those who, knowing God according to their light, have nevertheless turned away from truth to falsehood and from worship of the Creator to the service of idols.  The *arsenokoitai* (active homosexual sodomists) and *malakoi* (or catamites) are threatened with disinheritance from the Kingdom of God.  He infers that they are responsible for their actions because they are guilty of leaving (*aphentes*) the natural use of the women. Many writers uphold that the early Christians regarded such addiction to homosexual practices as a sign of national degeneration and the inevitable accompaniment of idolatry.

*The early Church*, as we have seen, entertained no doubt that Sodom and Gomorrah were destroyed by divine vengeance because of the cities' addiction to homosexual practices. Homosexual acts were condemned by the Fathers, however, not only on Biblical grounds, but also because they always regarded them as unnatural in themselves. *Tertullian* says that they are not so much sins as monstrosities and those who perpetrate them should be banished not only from the threshold but from all shelter of the Church. They are acts of frenzied lust and as such exceed the laws of nature, being dangerous not only to the human body but threatening the very structure itself of the sexes.[24]

*John Chrysostom* is particularly emphatic in denouncing homosexual practices as unnatural.[25] Commenting on Rom. i. 26-27 he holds that no one "can say that it was by being hindered of legitimate intercourse that they came to this pass, or that it was from having no means to fulfill their desire that they were driven into this monstrous insaneness". Women have no defence he writes and neither have men who "not only had the means of gratification, and left that which they had, and went after another [but] having dishonoured that which was natural they ran after that which was contrary to nature". All

---

[24] *De Pudic.* c. IV. PL. 2, 1032.
[25] *In epist. ad Rom.* IV. PG. 60, 415-22.

genuine pleasure is according to nature, but when God is excluded then "all things are turned upside down". Women are more blameworthy than the men as lesbianism is even more disgraceful. "And yet a more disgraceful thing than these is it, when even the women seek after these intercourses, who ought to have more sense of shame than men." All this is, for Chrysostom an evident proof "of the last degree of corruptness", since such people jeopardize the human race by deflecting the sexual organs from their primary procreative purpose, as well as sowing disharmony between man and woman. Both he—and she—work the deeds of enemies against one another. The sexes are divorced from one another so that they "become two parts in opposition to the law of God".

*Augustine* contends that homosexual practices are transgressions of the command to love God and one's neighbour, and declares that "those shameful acts such as were committed in Sodom, ought everywhere and always to be detested and punished. If all nations were to do such things they would [equally] be held guilty of the same crime by the law of God, which has not made that men should use one another in this way".[26] He considers sodomy a bodily defilement, and a lie is permissible to avoid being compelled to submit to it,[27] provided it does not violate "the doctrine of piety, nor piety itself, nor innocence, nor benevolence".[28]

*The Apostolic Constitution* vi. 28: stresses the unnaturalness of homosexual practices.

[26] *Conf. III.* viii (15) PL. 32. 689-90.
[27] *De Mend.* ix. PL. 40, 499.
[28] *Ibid.*, xx. PL. 40, 515-6.

"We believe that lawful marriage, and the begetting of children, is honourable and undefiled, for difference of sexes was formed in Adam and Eve for the increase of mankind. . . . We abhor all unlawful mixtures and that which is practised by some against nature as wicked and impious".[29] The conjunction of male and female is said to be acceptable to God's mind because the difference of sexes was established for the procreation of children. "But we do not say so of that mixture that is contrary to nature, or any unlawful practice, for such are an enmity to God. For the sin of Sodom is contrary to nature. . . . The practisers— attempt the dissolution of the world and endeavour to make the natural course of things to change for one that is unnatural."[30]

From even the most cursory examination of Patristic thought no one could deny that the early Church regarded homosexual practices as evil and deserving of condemnation. *This condemnation persists up to our own time and has remained unchanged throughout the ages.* At the beginning of the fourth century, the Council of Elvira (305-6) included a canon which forbade the admission of '*stupratores puerorum*' to Holy Communion, even when at death's door.[31] A few years later at the Council of Ancrya in Asia Minor (314) canons 16 and 17 were directed against those who were guilty of homosexual practices.[32]

In the East at the close of this century Basil wrote to Amphilochius, Bishop of Iconium, and laid down the following rule. Epist. ccxvii, can. 62. "He who is guilty of

---

[29] PL. I. 938.
[30] *Ibid.*, vi. 27-28; PG. I. 982-3.
[31] Conc. *Illib*, 71. *Sacrorum Conciliorum. Nova et Amplissima Collectio.* Mansi. ii. 17.
[32] *Conc. Ancyr* 16 & 17. *Ibid.*, ii. 518-9.

unseemliness with males (*tēn aschēmosunen en tois arr-hesin*) will be under discipline for the same time as adulterers."[33]    Gregory of Nyssa in his canonical letter to Letoius, Bishop of Melitene, probably written about 390, explains that his reason for treating sodomists the same way as adulterers is because both acts involve the commission of an injustice.[34]

During the following centuries the legislation against homosexual practices is mainly repetitive,ʻ so selected examples will suffice to show the general attitude of the Church.  At the famous Council of Naples (1120) twenty-five canons were directed against sins of the flesh, of which four were aimed specially at sodomists.[35]   The third Lateran Council (1179) warns against that incontinence "*quae contra naturam est, propter quam venit ira Dei in filios diffidentiae*",[36] and similar enactments are found later in the Council of Paris (1212),[37] and the Council of Rheims (1214).[38]   These laws clearly show that *ecclesiastical legislation condemned homosexual practices.*

A much more thorough treatment of the question of homosexuality is found in *the Penitentials*, where penances are graded according to the particular homosexual act committed.   While the Penitentials are noted for their realistic approach to the problem, they offer no

[33] PG. 32, 799-800.
[34] PG. 45. 277.
[35] Conc. Neapolit. 8, 9, 10, 11.   *Ibid.*, xxi. c. 264.
[36] Conc. III Lateran. Can. xi.   *Histoire des Conciles* (Paris, 1872) Héfèle. Tom. VII. pp. 504-5.
[37] Conc. Paris. ii. 21. *Mansi*, xxii. 831.
           iii. 2. *Ibid.*, xxii. 834.
[38] Conc. Rotomag. ii. 23, 32, *Ibid.*, xxii. 904-5.

explanation of their system, and no reason why one homosexual practice should merit a greater penalty than another. It would be a large and complicated task to give a complete synopsis of their penances relating to homosexual practices, yet a select account will suffice to convey the attitude of the Penitentials to homosexual practices.

All homosexual acts are held to be sinful in some measure and certain ones are regarded as specially grave.[39] There is discrimination between those who adopt the active and passive role;[40] between occasional and habitual indulgence;[41] and between first and subsequent offences.[42]

During *the Middle Ages* homosexual practices were regarded more from the aspect of their being *peccata contra naturam,* not that this element was hitherto ignored, but rather that it now received fuller treatment. The *Liber Gomorrhianus of Peter Damiani* was probably the most remarkable book on homosexual practices published at this time.[43] He discussed for the benefit of Pope Leo IX the different kinds of sins against nature, and the appropriate methods for dealing with those who indulged in them. For them all he has the harshest censures,[44] and in his opinion bestiality is less grave a lust than homosexual lust.[45] He laments over the fate of those souls who abandon themselves to such foul prac-

[39] A most comprehensive range of distinctions between homosexual acts is found in the Penitential of Cummean (7th century) ii. 8, 9, 10; x. 2, 3, 6, 7, 8, 9, 14, 16. ed. F. Wassernschleben, *Die Bussordungen der abendländischen Kirche* (Halle, 1851), pp. 460-93.

[40] *Ibid.*, x. 9.

[41] *Ibid.*, ii, 8; x, 7, 8, 16.

[42] *Ibid.*, x. 14.

[43] He was at that time head of a monastery of Fonte Avellana, near Gubbio.

[44] *Migne. PL.* 144, 161.

[45] *"Ut mihi videtur, tolerabilius est cum pecude quam cum viro in luxuriae flagitium labi."* *Ibid.,* 167.

tices,[46] and such conduct is heinous in a priest, for God will not accept any sacrifice from hands stained by filthy acts,[47] nor any oblation or sanctity which has been defiled by pollution.[48] He attacks the Penitentials for their lenient treatment in assigning inadequate punishment for homosexual offences,[49] and holds that every sin against nature deserves the maximum penalty.

*St. Thomas* discusses the subject of homosexual practices in detail when he deals with it in the course of the treatise on the cardinal virtue of temperance. One of the vices contrary to temperance, he says, is lust, the essence of which is that it "exceeds the order and mode of reason where venereal acts are concerned".[50] Discordance with right reason is present whenever something is done which is inconsistent with the proper end of such acts. This end is first of all the generation of children. Since the sin against nature in any form is directed solely to the pursuit of venereal pleasure and excludes procreation, it clearly offends against reason and must be considered as one of the species of lust.[51]

This particular vice has a distinguishing feature in that it is also "contrary to the natural order of the venereal act as becoming to the human race".[52] It is a *vitium contra naturam* and occurs in four ways:

    i. by masturbation;
    ii. by bestiality;
    iii. by *concubitus ad non debitum sexum*—coition with one of the same sex.
    iv. by deviation from the natural manner of coition.

[46] *Ibid.*, 177.     [47] *Ibid.*, 181.     [48] *Ibid.*, 183.     [49] *Ibid.*, 169-172.
[50] *Summa Theol.*, II-II, Q. cliii. 3; cf. Q. cliii. 2; Q. cliv. i.
[51] *Ibid.*, II-II, Q. cliv. i.     [52] *Ibid.*, II-II, Q. cliv. ii.

These four infringements cover by definition or by implication all forms of male and female homosexual
practice. Bestiality is stated to be the most grievous sin
against nature, next comes sodomy, then non-observance
of the *debitus modus concumbendi*, while masturbation is
regarded as the least serious.[53]  He regarded any of these
sins against nature as more sinful of its kind than any
other species of lust.

Aquinas also considers other relevant questions.  An
argument often used by homosexuals who wish to justify
their homosexual practices with another consenting adult
is that other sexual sins (adultery, rape and seduction) are
graver than the sin against nature since they injure one's
neighbour. Aquinas insists, however, that *any* transgres-
sion against nature is an injury to the Creator, whether or
not any offence is at the same time committed against
one's neighbour. All homosexual acts, therefore, are
transgressions of the Divine law which governs man's
sexual nature.[54]

Another point of interest in this connection concerns
other homosexual acts such as touches, caresses, and
kisses. Aquinas observes that such acts can be done without lustful pleasure and are therefore not mortally sinful
in themselves, but become so by reason of their motive.
They are lustful and therefore gravely sinful when they
are done for the purpose of enjoying forbidden pleasure
since consent to the pleasure of a lustful act is no less
sinful than consent to the act itself.[55]  Therefore even
when they do not lead to the commission of specific acts,

[53] *Ibid.*, II-II, Q. cliv. ad 4.
[54] *Summa Theol.*, II-II, Q. cliv. 12 ad i.
[55] *Ibid.*, II-II, Q. cliv. 4.

homosexual caresses and kisses for the purpose of venereal pleasure are condemned. Aquinas does not seem to condemn as lustful those acts which are simply expressions of regard or affection between persons of the same sex, provided they are not liable to arouse venereal excitement.

Finally in our consideration of the objective morality of homosexuality we examine the *relationship of homosexual acts to the nature of the sexual organs*. The purpose of coition may be described as conceptional and relational, the former destined for the procreation of children, and the latter for the establishment of the 'one flesh union' (*henōsis*). These purposes must never be separated so that one would exclude the other entirely and permanently. The use of the sexual organs, therefore, is significantly limited to an exclusive and lifelong relationship within the married state.

It is quite common to find practising homosexuals who claim their homosexual acts are their only means of expressing 'love' and thus the relational concept of coition is preserved. But, as we have said, the relational purpose must never be entirely and permanently separated, as would happen in homosexual coition. Homosexual 'love', may be compared in some way with various kinds of heterosexual 'love' (e.g. brother for sister) in so far as it has as its special distinguishing feature chastity, or the total exclusion of venereal acts.

Since there has been no change in the Church's attitude since the Medieval times, it would not be of any great benefit to follow her teaching through the succeeding centuries. It is accepted by all authorities that the condemnation of homosexual practices has never faltered throughout the years, and this constant belief has so dominated moral theology manuals, that the treatment of homosexual acts is exceedingly brief. From the teachings we have examined, therefore, *we hold that homosexual acts are intrinsically sinful and are peccata contra naturam*. They have been condemned by the Church not only because of the Sodom story, but also as the result of other clear Biblical references, the teaching of the Fathers, and the Councils of the Church. St. Thomas's condemnation of them on natural grounds is but the echo of the constant teaching of the Fathers especially St. John Chrysostom who in turn was influenced by St. Paul.

There is little or no assistance forthcoming *however as to the morality of the homosexual condition* except by implication. Heterosexuality is considered as the only sexual state and *positive sources had no reason to consider homosexuality other than a bad-habit fixation*. Indeed, as we shall see, the position today is still essentially unchanged.

# CHAPTER NINE

# The Mental and Moral Outlook
## of the Homosexual

THE moralist's problem with homosexuality lies more with the subjective rather than the objective morality. As always, subjective morality is more difficult to estimate than objective because of the many concrete, individual, cultural factors that enter into any judgement concerning subjective morality. While we appreciate that each individual case of homosexuality should receive its own particular judgement, nevertheless, we shall find it helpful if we can establish any general statements applicable to homosexuals as a group. We shall examine, therefore, the mental and moral approach of the homosexual at the moment when he becomes conscious of his anomaly.

Undoubtedly there are many homosexuals who for a variety of reasons remain all through their lives quite unaware of their sexual propensity towards their own sex. Case histories testify to the truth of this fact, though in such cases one cannot always rule out the possibility that the case is one of bisexualism rather than of true homosexuality. Many of these homosexuals have been known to marry and rear a family. Generally a happy well-adapted life is the greatest contributing factor to their ignorance of their sexual deviation. Due to the greater publicity given to the problem of homosexuality in recent times, many 'confirmed bachelors' may begin to suspect that they are abnormal in the direction of their sexual drive, while others who experience homosexual temptations will now begin to put a name to their anomaly. A man, for example, may strongly desire to marry, but is perplexed at his lack of interest in the physical relationship of marriage. He may now find the answer to his query, especially if he confesses that hitherto he has gravitated towards male company, even though no overt homosexual acts have actually taken place.

However deep-rooted his tendencies, the homosexual may become conscious of his inclinations only when he is initiated to homosexual practices, therein finding his emotions greatly stirred by a pleasurable sexual experience in a homosexual setting. In fact he may discover his homosexuality in any of the circumstances which would leave a normal man relatively unscathed. These circumstances have a deep emotional significance for him, and he now knows himself for what he is—a homosexual. He may have engaged in homosexual practices like other adolescents, but when they are adjusting themselves to the female world he finds that the woman is not the predominant figure in his psycho-sexual life. When the opportunity comes for associating more closely with women he recognizes that he is unable to enter into normal relations with them, so that the precipitating factor in his consciousness of his homosexual condition in such a case would be his contact with the opposite sex. He may have engaged previously in homosexual practices but felt that he could return to normal heterosexual life if and when he so desired, since the female was still the more sexually attractive to him. Gradually this latter attraction recedes into the background until the moment comes when he is more or less fixed in his homosexual bias.

At the moment of consciousness the homosexual will be influenced by many factors. His psycho-physical constitution, family background and, to a greater extent, the type of character he has formed for himself, aided by grace and freewill, will largely determine his mental attitude and moral approach to his homosexual condition. He may refrain in the future from all sexual activity if he is unable to assume a heterosexual orientation. On the other hand he may choose to yield to his instincts and indulge to the extent allowed him by his *home-made moral code* or give himself over to his inclinations without any restrictions whatsoever. We shall first of all consider his approach to his condition, and later to its expression in homosexual acts.

In the homosexual condition the following types or patterns of conduct may arise. (*a*) He may will to change and become heterosexual at whatever the cost. (*b*) Or he may feel unable to will a change, either because of his distrust in the efficacy of an attempted cure, or because he is afraid of the consequences involved in heterosexuality. (*c*) Or he may be content to remain as he is in a state which he feels is desirable.

The first type of homosexual will accept the truth about himself and his condition, and this knowledge generally brings with it a feeling of shame and is a time of great confusion. He realizes that he must be willing to fight himself, and the period of his struggle may be a long arduous one depending on the strength of his homosexual tendencies.

"It is a hand-to-hand struggle against the old and repeated faults of an education stifled by puritanism and by prudery, woven through the meshes of parental complexes and neuroses."[1]

The second type is the conscious homosexual who may be gripped by a fatalism that it is impossible for him to be other than he is. In such an event, even though he may wish to be otherwise, he feels he cannot really will it; mainly because he distrusts the efficacy of a cure, and is not prepared to undergo the long treatment necessary to make him a normal heterosexual.

The third type feels unequal to the contest involved in attaining heterosexuality, and leaves the field of battle in his own soul, resigning himself to his homosexual condition with the fear that one day he may yield to his tendencies. He is afraid to go out to the unknown—the heterosexual state. One of the characteristics often attributed to homosexuality is that of narcissism.

"For the homosexual the discovery will be to find himself again in another being; his joy will be to recognize in another his own reflection scarcely altered: his security finally, will consist in being able to read in his partner, without the effort of transposition from one mode to another, the answer already anticipated because it is merely a simple echo of his question."[2]

The *narcissistic homosexual* lives in a certain psychological isolation and it is extremely difficult to establish any form of sympathetic contact with him. We believe, from our study of the problem, that there is a strong narcissistic element in homosexuality, and this is evidenced in the

[1] *New Problems in Medical Ethics*, pp. 88.
[2] *Ibid.*, p. 112.

manner in which the homosexual clings to the adolescent concept of love which is primarily a communion of souls. He visualizes a David-and-Jonathan friendship as the only example of true love. His concept of love has gone astray, and he attempts to love with the soul one who loves him in the same manner. He does not belong to the outside world, lest in giving himself to others he loses contact with himself. Failing to admit in his own case the concept of heterosexual love, he indulges in self-centredness which he believes is best realized in the homosexual state.

Fr. Larère shows the portrayal of this type of homosexual love in Giraudoux's book *Sodom et Gomorrhe* where the inhabitants of Sodom having opted for inverted love are assembled according to sex.

"The woman, Lia, then voices her sentiments of love for the other women who share her bed: 'You are trembling, you are shivering with cold my little Ruth? Ah no? You tremble with fear. So much the better. I have always longed to have my sentiments, not in my heart, but beside me, in a being like to myself whom I can hug and caress. Come to me, Ruth, that I may caress my fear. Come, Judith, that I may embrace my sweetness, my frailty. . . . Oh, what a beautiful mirror belongs at last to myself'. . . . Here is indeed the mirror of Narcissus."[3]

It frequently happens that such a homosexual belongs to the next category; the man who is content to remain as he is, in a state which he feels is desirable, especially if he regards it as an integral part, if not an enrichment, of his personality.

There are times when this type of homosexual would posi-

[3] *New Problems in Medical Ethics*, p. 112.

tively resist any attempt to make him heterosexual. He has come to terms with his deviation and for him the important thing is to remain homosexual, not only because of the pleasure he derives from any homosexual acts in which he may indulge, but because the homosexual way of life is attractive to him. He would hardly want to remain a homosexual if he did not find it attractive. He generally seems unable to cope with the fears of a lonely life bereft of the happiness which he finds in the homosexual setting.

In both of these two latter categories, however, it must be realized that the homosexual is often motivated by vague egocentric impulses rather than by rational thought. It is often weakness of will as much as any conscious rationalizing that prevents these two types from placing themselves in the first category. This, as we shall see later on, is of great practical significance in the pastoral approach to the problem.

*The obvious error involved in homosexuality lies in the homosexual's false concept of human love.* As in all errors, where definite steps are taken, a certain progression sets in. The homosexual who accepts his homosexual condition as inevitable has three courses open to him as regards the actual expression of his homosexual propensity: he may abstain completely from all sexual acts; he may allow himself certain liberties legitimized by his own home-made moral code; or he may impose no limits on his homosexual conduct and refuse to be guided by any code, objective or subjective.

If he adopts the first course he accepts that no homosexual practices are permitted even to those in his condition who are not in any way conscious of being responsible for the homosexual fixation. Such a chaste man generally has strong religious convictions.

Others, however, refuse to acknowledge the limitations imposed on them by the moral law. Upholding the fallacy that sexual acts are necessary for the development of personality, they contend that it is lawful for them to commit certain homosexual acts which are 'natural' to people in their condition. Professing the irreversibility of their homosexuality, they formulate a home-made moral code by which they seek to legitimize, at least for themselves, certain types of homosexual acts. As regards the repeal of the law punishing consenting adult homosexuals, we would like to point out that the step from justification in the legal sphere to that of the moral justification of homosexual liaisons is a slight one, that has already been taken by many professed homosexual writers who thus attempt to salve their 'moral consciences'.

It would be impossible in the scope of this work to follow in detail the intricacies of the rationalizations involved in the formulation of these subjective codes, which take on various facets dependent on the individual concerned. One thing is certain, however, to which case histories clearly testify, that even though in the beginning the homosexuals may only desire friendship, or love without sex, such homosexual liaisons usually culminate at a genital level. This may become the predominant, if not the only, pleasure sought in the other's company. This frequent degeneration and swift disintegration of the practising homosexual's code underlines the unnaturalness of his rejection of the true moral code. 'Love' may be asked for at the outset of the partnership, and there may be no conscious intention of seeking homosexual practices, but, as is evident from the following selected cases, homosexual acts will manifest themselves sooner or later as the expression of mutual affection. The first case is of a clerk of twenty-two years, who testifies that

"it always works out the same way. I start by admiring them [men] from a distance, and wanting to get friendly with them. I'm sure that I don't think about sex to start with, but as I get to know them, the urge to possess them gets stronger and stronger until at last I have to do something about it. . . . Each time I fall in love with a man, I really want him as a friend. I really don't know why I have to go and spoil it all."[4]

The testimony of a doctor, who was serving a sentence of sixteen years for bank robbery, explains

"how his attraction for another young inmate degenerated to a base level. . . . At first it was only a liking for him, but it increased all the time, till I couldn't think of any woman. . . . For two years I loved him without the slightest taint of sex desire. It was the purest affection I ever felt in my life. It was all-absorbing, and I would have sacrificed my life for him if he had asked it. But by degrees the psychic stage began to manifest all the expressions of love between the opposite sexes. . . . I passed through every phase of a passionate love. With this difference, though—I felt a touch of the old disgust at the thought of actual sex contact. That I didn't do. It seemed to me a desecration of the boy, and of my love for him. But after a while that feeling also wore off, and I desired sexual relation with him."[5]

[4] *Society and the Homosexual*, p. 138.
[5] *Ibid.*, pp. 134-5.

There are other home-made codes which allow physical contact, but within certain arbitrary limits imposed by their authors, as is shown by the following case-history.

A successful business-man of forty-two testifies that he

" will not have sexual relations with another man unless four conditions are fulfilled.

1. He must be an avowed homosexual, but not living with, or in love with anyone else.
2. He must be over twenty-three.
3. He will only indulge in mutual masturbation.  He considers any other form of sexual activity to be perverted.
4. He discourages affection from his partner, and if he finds he is getting too fond of a man, he breaks off the relationship.

He does not object to paying a prostitute provided these four conditions are fulfilled. . . .   He admits that this code is unusual. . . .   He says that he would prefer to have one regular partner but he has not found anyone who shares his own ethical and moral code."[6]

This need for contact with those of his own sex can take many forms, as is shown by the following case of a young teacher, who testifies that

" carnal temptation comes and often takes the form of a quest for something or other; the contact, the presence of and intimacy with other people . . . I indulge all kinds of secret folly which can bring me nearer to them [his pupils] from every point of view: indiscretions, seeking for intimate notes, or again more carnal contacts, their linen— to the extent of making myself stupid, ridiculous."[7]

[6] *Ibid.*, p. 152.
[7] *New Problems in Medical Ethics*, p. 73.

In his case there will come a time when he will crave even still more carnal contacts, and so begin the seduction of his pupils.

Perhaps the most common pattern, particularly among the younger homosexuals, is that which starts off in a burst of idealism when two men believe that they are in love with each other and live together in a state which they regard as analogous to marriage. This they justify as the only form of 'matrimony' open to them, thus warping the Church's counsels that people who have not the gift of continence should marry. They say they have not the gift of continence and so the Church counsels them to marry each other!

But this falsely idealistic pattern seldom lasts, since the analogy with marriage is too forced and unrealistic. All too soon a pattern very familiar in homosexual circles is followed; occasional infidelities become habitual on one or both sides, and after a period of stormy recriminations and neurotic depressions they will either part company, or, as sometimes happens where there are common interests apart from sex, they may continue to share the same establishment on a 'semi-detached' basis, each going his own way in his quest for an increasing variety of sexual experience. Exceptions to this disintegration are rare indeed, but apparently not unknown, and such exceptions are the dream of many an idealistic homosexual. It is to be deplored that such false partnership should be presented in certain types of homosexual literature as being of frequent occurence.

This idealistic type of homosexual, however, condemns paederasty and male prostitution with as much vehemence as he attacks adultery and fornication. It is doubtful, though, if he is as sincere as he appears, or really as satisfied with his own moral arrangements as he pretends. *His unhappiness comes, not from the condemnation of society as such, but from his unnatural approach to the laws governing sexual practices.* His Honour J. Tudor Rees, formerly Chairman of Ṣurrey Quarter Sessions, says:

> "It is certainly my experience . . . that nearly all homosexuals I have known have been emotionally unbalanced and profoundly unhappy. I do not believe that this is solely or exclusively due to the fear of detection, or the sense of guilt attaching itself to practices disapproved of by society. It is inherent in the nature of an activity for which the bodily organs employed are physically unsuited."[8]

Previously, the homosexual may have committed homosexual acts without seeking to justify them. This self-justification is ordinarily psychologically decisive in the life of the homosexual who accepts his homosexual propensity as the result of a fatal instinct. Normal in the greater part of his life, he had, as it were, a homosexual world apart which he visited from time to time, but his whole life was not under the sway of his homosexual instincts. Now the homosexual milieu becomes more necessary for him, and he becomes obsessed with the fear that his two worlds might suddenly collide and that he would become known for what he was.

The homosexual realizes that the future holds nothing but loneliness for him, and eventually he generally jettisons all pretence at self-justification and makes no attempt to exercise any self-control. He becomes notoriously self-indulgent, ignoring the fact that there are many hetero-

[8] *They Stand Apart*, pp. 25-6.

sexuals who, because of some physical defect or other disability, are denied the use of their sexual functions.

Finally there is the homosexual who imposes no limits or moral code upon himself. He is dominated by his homosexual condition and his homosexual acts. His life is punctuated by homosexual partnerships of varying lengths of time. His condition colours the least of his attitudes, and he is immediately known and just as spontaneously greets another like himself. He is generally anti-social and attempts to blame others for his immoral failings, striving with all his power to break society, simulating contempt for the normal in order to offset his own inferiority complex.[9] Yet all his arrogance is nothing more than a defence against his feelings of insecurity and doubt. Ostracizing himself from society, he looks upon sexual intimacy as the only way to fill the void of loneliness largely caused by himself. Unable to ignore society, he wages war on all moral standards as his only way to bridge the gap between himself and normal men.

In passing we may mention that great importance has been attached by many writers to *the significance of the role taken by the practising homosexual, whether active or passive.* Fundamentally, from a scientific point of view, we believe that the role itself is not as important as the state of mind which conditions it. While it is true, as a general rule, that the masculine type is the active partner, this is not an infallible criterion. It is much more common to find practising homosexuals engaging in active

[9] *Society and the Homosexual*, p. 151.
" Beneath the façade of contentment . . . many homosexuals are not inwardly at peace with themselves. The so-called well-adjusted homosexual is often not without conflict which he may learn to conceal by bravado or express in his contempt for conventionality." *Ibid.*, p. 140.

and passive roles alternately, even with the same partner, apparently irrespective of physical constitution. Such preferences, if present, are mainly due to circumstances and opportunity.

In conclusion then we believe that the homosexual who permits himself certain indulgences, is not as subjectively convinced as he pretends, and his arrogance is a mask to cover his intense feelings of unhappiness and insecurity. This is due to the unnaturalness of his acts of which he is aware, rather than attributable to the condemnation of society.

# CHAPTER TEN

# Moral Responsibility

~~~~~~~~~~~~~~~~~~~~~~~~~~~~~~~~~~~~~~~~~~~~~~~~~~~~~~~~~~

## I. THE HOMOSEXUAL CONDITION

In previous chapters we have examined the various theories which are supposed to explain the causation of the homosexual propensity, and in the light of these modern scientific experiments we shall consider whether and to what extent the homosexual is responsible for his condition and his homosexual practices. Any theory holding that the sexual drive is predetermined independently of the conscious choice of the subject will necessarily exonerate the homosexual from all responsibility for the origin of his condition. His particular bias would then be so fixed that he has very little possibility of re-directing it. The first problem, therefore, is whether or not the homosexual has any responsibility for his condition. To solve it we shall answer the following four questions:

(a) Is homosexuality a natural alternative to heterosexuality?
(b) Is homosexuality a constitutional and therefore natural variation?
(c) Is homosexuality a physical or psychological disease?
(d) Is homosexuality a bad-habit fixation?

*(a) Is homosexuality a natural alternative to hetero-sexuality?*

Many authorities regard it as such, owing its origin and growth to the same psycho-physical factors. They contend that the homosexual is such by the will of God and is no more to be blamed for the direction of his sexual drive than the heterosexual is to be praised for the normality of his sexual impulses. Such a theory, we hold contradicts not only revealed truth but also the conclusions of reason on which are based systems of human law. Except for the fact that homosexuals exist—otherwise our problem could not arise—there is nothing whatever to suggest that the natural and divinely ordained human condition is other than *uniquely heterosexual*. Present available medical evidence gives overwhelming support to the condemnation of the "alternative sexual state theory", and equally rejects the intersexuality of the homosexual condition, thereby refuting the theory which regards the homosexual as a *tertium quid* between male and female.

*(b) Is homosexuality a constitutional and therefore natural variation?*

Many biologists hold that homosexuality, like other physical defects such as blindness, is found constantly recurring in a minority of the human race. The homosexual should not feel any guilt about his condition just as he would not blame himself were he colour-blind. We hold, however, that while there is medical evidence for the innate constitutional character of other physical defects, none is available for the homosexual condition. What positive medical evidence there is argues strongly against the hypothesis, and in fact provides little or nothing to substantiate a medical origin to the deviation. Even though the investigation into cases of similar twins admittedly suggests that a medical factor, at present unknown, cannot be altogether excluded, nevertheless the results so far published do not give solid ground for reversing our verdict.

### (c) Is homosexuality a physical or psychological disease?

But even though homosexuality may not justly be regarded as a natural deviation, the possibility still remains that the condition may be the outcome of some disease. Some doctors look upon the homosexual as a sick person who constitutes an exclusively medical problem. The afflicted person has little or no control over his malady which completely or in large part causes his sexual deviation. Yet, we have shown that even the most cursory examination of the British Medical Association's Report openly reveals the inadequacy of available medical data to explain homosexuality on a biological or endocrinological basis. The Report does not even visualize the possibility that all cases of homosexuality have a medical background It is true that medical symptoms are claimed to be present in a minority of cases. But these symptoms are merely said *to dispose* the individual to form heterosexual relationships. If a person, therefore, does become fixed in his homosexuality, it is implied that there are other causative factors inducing the more or less permanent nature of his condition.[1] Consequently if he is not to be held responsible for the direction of his sexual drive, he cannot claim this exemption on purely medical grounds.

[1] *Op. cit.*, p. 27.

M

The Wolfenden Report, too, rejects the "disease theory" since it fulfils none of the three conditions required for a disease.[2] These *conditions consist of (a) abnormal symptoms*, which (*b*) must be *caused by a demonstrable pathological condition*, and (*c*) *this in turn must find its explanation in some factor or factors called the 'cause'*. "Homosexuality," writes the Wolfenden Committee, "does not satisfy any of them unless the terms in which they are defined are extended beyond what could reasonably be regarded as legitimate."[3]

As regards the first condition—*the presence of abnormal symptoms*—homosexuality cannot be regarded as a disease "because in many cases it is the only symptom, and is compatible with full mental health in other respects".[4] It is extremely rash to assume that aberrant behaviour is necessarily symptomatic of disease. This would be to extend illegitimately the concept of illness and restrict that of moral failure. If psychiatric disorders are present in a number of homosexual cases, it will be found that they are generally explainable as the outcome rather than the cause of the homosexual condition. They are the products of the emotional strain and conflict set up by the homosexual propensity and not its causal factors.

Some cases of mental illness are accompanied by *a demonstrable physical pathology*, the second condition demanded in the Report. The Committee feel, however, that as regards this second criterion of disease, "we have heard no convincing evidence that this has yet been demonstrated in relation to homosexuality".[5] Our examination of biochemical and endocrine studies has proved

[2] *Op. cit.*, p. 15.     [4] *Ibid.*, p. 14.
[3] *Ibid.*, p. 14.        [5] *Ibid.*, p. 15.

negative, and other methods, such as the investigation of body-build, fail to establish any relationship between homosexuality and a demonstrable physical pathology. The so-called psychopathological theories adduced for homosexuality have also been found recurring in others besides the homosexual. These hypotheses have no verifiable basis in observed facts, and therefore cannot enter into the formation of an objective moral judgement on the homosexual condition.

As regards the third criterion, *the cause,* there is never one single cause for normal or abnormal behaviour, mental health or illness. Any number of physical or environmental elements, therefore, may have been instrumental in producing the homosexual condition. Owing partly to the inadequateness of the research into the homosexual condition, none of these elements which we have investigated—genetic predisposition, unbalanced family relationships, segregation, faulty sex education— can be proved to bear a specific causal relationship to any recognized psychopathology or physical pathology. The Wolfenden Report states that "to assert a direct or specific causal relationship between these factors and the homosexual condition is to ignore the fact that they have all, including seduction, been observed to occur in persons who become entirely heterosexual in their disposition".[6] *Homosexuality, therefore, is most certainly not a disease.*

### (d) Is homosexuality a bad-habit fixation?

There remains to be considered the question of homosexuality as a bad-habit fixation. In this section we are

[6] *Op cit.,* p. 15.

not considering whether the homosexual suffers from a condition which causes diminished responsibility for his sexual behaviour, but whether and to what extent he was responsible in the past for the origin of his present sexual deviation. Homosexuality is present in different individual homosexuals, and there are no grounds for regarding the condition as irrevocably fixed in every case to such an extent as to exclude any possibility of the emergence of normal heterosexuality. It is more in line with the facts to regard it as an emotional disaster the roots of which lie in a false concept of human love. This intellectual aberration grows more difficult to displace the longer it is left unchallenged, and its strength increases when fostered by internal and external acts. The stage will therefore arise where the dominant sexual drive is homosexual in character. From this it would seem that there are no positive reasons for a refusal to consider the condition as anything more than a bad-habit fixation. However, if this were so, the same determining value would have to be attributed to physical and psychological factors as in other such fixations. These factors may reasonably be held to produce a corresponding diminuation of responsibility in regulating the direction of the sexual drive.

In estimating the moral responsibility of the homosexual condition, there is an important element that cannot be disregarded. The theologian calls it *concupiscence* and often intends to signify a moral disorder connoting the failure of the will to control the activity of the sensitive appetites and instincts. Here, however, we would rather regard it more neutrally as the spontaneous movements of these appetites and instincts in so far as they anticipate man's reason. It is imperative that at this stage reason should intervene to control these movements so that what-ever action results will be morally right. If there is no attempt made to control these instinctive movements of sense, then the habitual reaction will be to give a preponderating influence to the desires consequent upon them in any decision the subject may be called on to make. His conduct acquires a certain compulsion so that in due course a bad-habit is effectively installed.

When conduct is not consciously premeditated, ob-viously a man, carried away by the passion of the moment, is judged as not fully responsible for his actions. But he may well be judged blameworthy by his failure to over-come vicious propensities of whose existence he is fully aware. No one has the right to expose himself to the danger of the effects of a sudden burst of passion without a serious reason. These principles are fully applicable to a man conscious of his homosexual tendencies. When, however, he deliberately chooses to remain as he is—with all its consequent dangers—then his responsibility for his conduct is greatly increased. He is not innocent of blame for his actual condition and its consequences.

However, it is often impossible to establish a practical criterion which would infallibly separate the homosexual who is completely or in part responsible for the origin of his condition from those who are such through no fault of their own. We believe that each case must be con-sidered on its merits, and the responsibility, like the condition itself, is not an 'all or none' judgement. When more evidence comes to light we may be in a position to give more precise rules. For the moment it is of the utmost importance to remember that spontaneous homo-sexual desires, while they may exercise some influence on an individual's deliberate choice, are not of such a nature, in most cases at least, as to exert such compulsion as forces the person to actively will a homosexual condition.

The homosexuals responsibility, however, may be lessened on the grounds of *ignorance*. This further factor must be considered before the moral imputability of the homosexual for his condition is finally and rightly assessed. The homosexual condition, as we have seen, generally lies in varying degrees within the sphere of moral judgement, and is an aberration in the sexual sphere. Yet the homosexual would not be culpable if, for example, through no fault of his own, he was unaware that to desire willingly the homosexual condition itself is morally wrong, either because it has never occurred to him to enquire, or because, despite all reasonable attempts to gain enlightenment, he remains convinced that it is right. Does the homosexual fully understand the import of homosexuality? Some hold that the homosexual is, as a general rule, ignorant of the real meaning of human love and apparently incapable of understanding it. From this an erroneous conscience could follow, *a conscience, however, which must be informed and educated.*

There are certain basic moral principles, however, concerning which ignorance is not to be presumed. We believe that the unnaturalness of the homosexual condition belongs to this category, especially when it is realized that the homosexual is usually not as happy with his condition as he appears to be, nor as personally convinced by his own arguments as he would have others believe. This unhappiness follows, not so much from the condemnation of society as such, but from the unnaturalness of his whole attitude to life,[7] and therefore *until the contrary is proved, it must be held that the homosexual is fully aware of what he chooses to be or remain.*

Whether he is to be excused of blame on the grounds of supposed ignorance will depend largely on the extent to which he has sought enlightenment. If he has deliberately avoided enquiry into the morality of his condition lest he might feel compelled to undergo a long tedious cure and relinquish his attractive homosexual way of life, then such ignorance cannot be considered invincible. Neither is he excused if he failed to heed reasonable doubts that may have arisen at *various times of his life.* This latter fact is very important as homosexuality is progressive and is strengthened by further consenting acts of the will.

The priest must beware of the self-defence mechanism of the homosexual by which he attempts to justify himself for choosing to remain in his condition. Even though the psycho-sexual attraction towards the same sex may well be basically the result of circumstances outside the control of the individual concerned, nevertheless such a person cannot will to remain homosexual, as that is contrary to God's plan for mankind. He is bound *subgravi* to renounce his condition by a definite act of the will, and acknowledge the fact that his anomaly is more than an anomaly. It is a disorder and deviation, and the homosexual must will to adjust his life accordingly. However, it must be remembered that even though he may *will* to be otherwise he still feels the heterosexual way of life *unattractive.* An act of the will cannot change the attrac-

---

[7] The ill-concealed unhappiness of the homosexual was discussed in the previous chapter.

tiveness of the homosexual way of life, and the homosexual must not despair because homosexual desires remain as strongly entrenched as they were before he formally renounced them by an act of will. A further constituent of the moral judgement to be applied to the homosexual condition is the intrinsically evil nature of the object of homosexual desires, and the homosexual is morally blameworthy when he deliberately wills his homosexual desires.

However, the case is not infrequent where the homosexual is not seriously tempted to indulge his tendencies, and these will most probably remain after he has renounced his condition. But if he keeps his moral standards high, and has a satisfying vocation in life, he will scarcely be tempted to give way to such tendencies. He will accept heterosexuality as the condition willed by God for mankind even though this state may hold no attraction for him. In spite of his anomaly he may well be a model of Christian virtue in other respects, and be an example of selfless dedication to the service of others. To attempt a heterosexual orientation to his life would not seem to be spiritually profitable. His only fault may well have been too easy an acceptance of his homosexual condition. We do not think that in such a special case he has any obligation to undergo special medical or psychiatric treatment, given the small possibility of success, to achieve heterosexualization.[8]

In conclusion, therefore, it is our considered opinion that, after a careful examination of the main factors in-

___

[8] The questionable efficacy of medical and psychiatric treatment, and the doubtfully ethical methods so often employed, raise a new problem to which one at the moment is not able to provide a satisfactory answer.

volved, there can be no doubt that the homosexual is generally in some degree responsible for his condition, either for its origin, or at least willing to remain as he is. However, since there are many kinds of homosexuals, the degree of responsibility will vary with the individual. Each homosexual therefore has the right to offer in his defence the concrete circumstances that he believes led to his deviation.

## II. HOMOSEXUAL ACTS

Since the homosexual is responsible in some measure for his condition, there can be little doubt that he will bear yet more responsibility for its expression in internal and external acts. In terms of objective morality—that is, according to the standards of right reason—homosexual acts are intrinsically sinful. Biblical and Patristic sources regard them as an 'abomination' because they involve the reversal of what is sexually natural. Homosexuality, as we have said, is a moral problem just as any other sexual problem. We must distinguish therefore between the objective morality of the homosexual act and *the moral responsibility of the practising homosexual.* How far then may one say the latter is responsible for what he does?

It does not follow necessarily from the abnormality of the homosexual drive that the homosexual is *ipso facto* more frustrated than the heterosexual.[9] A very false emphasis has been put on this sense of frustration by irresponsible writers, and we condemn absolutely those who gratuitously hold that the homosexual is no longer a free

[9] The Wolfenden Report, p. 16.

agent when it comes to keeping his tendencies under control. The Wolfenden Committee also agrees with this judgement and says that homosexual impulses are not any less resistible than heterosexual.[10]  Just as in other moral spheres, there exists, *in a small minority of cases*, the practising homosexual who is a psychopath or suffers from some neurotic disorder.  The extent of his psychological disorder in so far as it curtails his freedom will measure his moral responsibility.  Again some writers plead that the loneliness of the homosexual is an important diminishing factor in his culpability especially when he begins to understand with the passage of time that the future holds an even bleaker prospect than he had hitherto realized.  In such cases we cannot in any way accept the underlying contention that every homosexual must be regarded as one suffering from a permanent anxiety state.  Sympathy must never displace truth in circumstances such as these where the exceptional case tends to become the rule.  In many respects the chaste homosexual is no lonelier than other celibates and we must constantly insist that the homosexual must adapt himself to his limitations in a life of chastity.[11]  The homosexual is generally as mentally healthy as a normal man and therefore the usual moral standards must be applied to his sexual activities.

There are certain homosexuals, however, who justify limited homosexual practices as morally legitimate for those in their condition as being their only means of ex-

[10] *Ibid.*, p. 16.

[11] " There are many heterosexual people who, because they suffer from physical defect or other disability, have to adapt their lives to their own limitations and the case of these homosexuals is not really different or more difficult." *Homosexuality and Prostitution*, p. 13.

pressing 'love'. Such a homosexual might argue that homosexual acts between consenting adults in private are less social evils than fornication and adultery. This defence mechanism of the moralizing homosexual is soon pierced, and it is quickly obvious that the homosexual is conscious of the sinfulness of his homosexual practices. When questioned, these homosexuals show a very great lack of appreciation of the real meaning of morality and theorise to suit their purpose while feigning moral indignation at other immoral practices of society.

The most common question proposed by the penitent homosexual concerns his responsibility for his sexual lapses once he has renounced his homosexual condition. If he is seriously endeavouring to break the habit of sinning, then the subsequent inadvertent acts done in consequence of the force of habit are not imputable in themselves as sinful. Since the habit is involuntary, then the acts issuing from it, if they are inadvertent, must be considered involuntary. This is merely theoretical, however, since it is practically impossible to prove this inadvertence in cases where homosexual acts take place with another, especially where sodomy is committed. In practice the homosexual may very well advert to his homosexual practices and consent to their commission. He is responsible for such acts but this responsibility will be diminished according to the force which habit still exercises over his intellect and will. The confessor, in his attempts to form a just estimate of this responsibility, must be guided in his judgement by the same considerations which he uses in other cases of sexual bad habits.

If the homosexual condition has not been deliberately renounced by the will, then voluntarily to foster, retain, or refuse to relinquish the bad habit in so far as in him lies, will necessarily increase the homosexual's guilt. *Even where he is not responsible for the origin of his condition, to accept such deviation voluntarily is to render himself responsible for what results from it.* Case-histories of practising homosexuals clearly demonstrate that the homosexual generally neglects to render his homosexual habit a remote occasion of sin. In so far as his inadvertent acts are concerned, his culpability is restricted to his neglecting to rid himself of his habit. Though this is theoretically true, evidence suggests that homosexual acts are voluntary, especially when they involve another party.

## CONCLUSIONS

From the investigations narrated in the foregoing chapters, we consider the following general principles are fully justified by the evidence. When this book was first envisaged, there was never any intention of fitting the facts to ready-made conclusions. That intention has been maintained throughout, and we cannot be accused of approaching this difficult subject emotionally or with undesirable subjectivity. Nor have our conclusions been inferences from the so-called "die-hard stubbornness of abstract morality", but have been solidly based on scientific facts made available in the twentieth century. Realizing the difficulties involved in assessing moral responsibility in the tangled homosexual skein, we shall confine ourselves to five general principles which give the real, and not idealized, picture of the homosexual's moral responsibility with regard to his condition and practices. We are aware that in the moral evaluation of any human action consideration must be shown to the individual, but this must be set in the framework of his real situation as a member of human society.

The followers of 'situation ethics' accuse us of building our morality round essential man, who does not exist, while they claim to base their morality on existential man, that is, man as he exists here and now. We know only too well the disastrous results this 'new morality' has caused among certain churchmen in England. The late Pope Pius XII pointed out that there can be no contradiction between essential and existential man since man's essence is not destroyed by his existence.[12] Taking all the circumstances of the situation into consideration we have examined the homosexual of today, and accordingly come to the following conclusions:

1. *The homosexual may not will to remain in the homosexual condition* since homosexuality as a state or *condition* is contrarily opposed to the natural and divinely ordained heterosexual state. This is true irrespective of whether or not the homosexual is responsible for the *origin* of his sexual deviation. However, we must reassert that an act of will cannot change the attractiveness of the homosexual way of life. Such a person must not think that this attraction is necessarily sinful. It becomes so only when he deliberately wills the homosexual desires which arise spontaneously. In some cases the homosexual is 'conditioned' prior to any act of his own will, nevertheless, as a general rule, he is also responsible in varying degrees for the origin of his homosexual propensity. Many

[12] Acta Apostolicae Sedis. XLV, (May 25-30, 1954), pp. 278-86.

factors, especially the influence of passion or his own ignorance, will determine the degree of his responsibility. Even though in some exceptional cases a state of invincible ignorance appears to be present, an investigation of the homosexual's attitude to his condition reveals a 'false defence', hence the added necessity of positive proof before he can be acquitted of moral guilt.

2. *Where the condition is recognized as a bad-habit proximately disposing to sin, it must be renounced effectively by the will,* i.e., with the resolve to do everything possible to diminish its power and to eradicate it as a habit which involves great danger of sin. This is a *grave obligation* since homosexual acts are intrinsically evil and at least grave material sins. In cases where homosexual tendencies are not over-dominant, this grave obligation can be fulfilled by a change of milieu, but where this is insufficient other measures should be taken. Unfortunately there is relatively little available evidence as to the efficacy of medical or psychiatric treatment.

3. *The homosexual is as capable of controlling the expression of his sexual drive as the heterosexual.* His moral responsibility must not be considered as essentially different from that of victims of other sexual bad habits. He is generally aware of what he does, and is generally cognizant of the fact that homosexual acts are sinful.

4. Where the homosexual condition has been positively and effectively renounced by the will there will be responsibility for the advertent acts which follow, but it will be diminished according to the force which the formally renounced habit still exercises. As a general rule some responsibility must be presumed for such acts.

5. Where no attempt has been made to renounce the

homosexual condition, there will be some responsibility for even inadvertent results of this state, especially when they are foreseen as likely to occur. But in general sufficient advertence is present to make these acts fully voluntary, particularly when another party is involved.

# CHAPTER ELEVEN

# The Priest and the Homosexual

GENERALLY speaking, it was rarer in the past for a priest to encounter homosexuality and its problems in the course of his ministry than it is today. He might learn occasionally about homosexual practices through the confessional, or he might be consulted from time to time by parents or headmasters about cases concerning boys. Again his priestly work may have occupied him in the educational formation of adolescents. We have already considered the question of the incidence of homosexuality today, but whether or not it is on the increase, recent publicity has so focused attention on the subject that civil authorities and homosexuals themselves turn more frequently to the Catholic Church for guidance and counsel. What should be the attitude of the priest to the homosexual, who confesses that his sexual bias is towards those of his own sex?

The most noticeable distinguishing mark of the Catholic Church is its optimism, which is in sharp contrast to the fatalistic and secularistic attitude of modern writers who stress the irreversibility of the homosexual propensity and its inevitable actual expression in homosexual practices. Yet the Church's optimism is tempered with an almost earthy realism about sin, gained from her long experience of fallen human nature. Catholic Theology alone gives man the *full truth* about his nature, his supernatural destiny, and the means which he must use to attain his goal. It offers constructive measures for the avoidance of homosexual acts. The homosexual by his homosexual practices is turning away from his supernatural end, although he may be completely unaware of it, he is morally sick and needs the spiritual guidance of the priest. Even on the purely natural plane, the problem of homosexuality is simplified when approached from the moral aspect. Since the homosexual is not inexorably determined by physical or psychical factors, fatalism can be broken and the possibility of a complete cure can sometimes be envisaged by the homosexual himself. Failing this, the priest can convince him that with God's grace he can at least bring his tendencies under control.

*Homosexuality should receive essentially the same pastoral treatment as other sexual problems.* Even though there is no outlet for the homosexual comparable to marriage, in other respects he is no different from the heterosexual. Therefore in this chapter we only concern ourselves with those aspects peculiar to the homosexual pattern. Apart from these specific suggestions, the homosexual should be treated by the priest in the same way as heterosexuals confronted with their sexual problems.

### I. THE PRIEST

What should be the *attitude of the priest* to the homosexual? All authors stress the need for a successful 'rapport'. This sympathetic attitude, creating to the

N

fullest possible extent an atmosphere of confidence, is a *condicio sine qua non* of an effective spiritual cure. Displaying no sign of embarrassment or disgust, the priest should preserve the sympathetic and non-censorious attitude that he shows to others. Some priests betray such emotional revulsion when confronted with the homosexual that they seem unfitted by temperament to effect the required remedial 'rapport'. Others assume a harsh attitude of bitter condemnation, while still more, although sympathetic, are convinced that nothing can be done. These attitudes are soon transmitted to the homosexual, who as a general rule is hyper-sensitive. Dissemination of knowledge as to the true character of homosexuality should produce a greater understanding of the homosexual and his special problems. The priest should equip himself with all the necessary information which will put the homosexual at his ease and contribute towards convincing him that the priest is in a position to help.[1]

In cases, however, where the priest feels frankly unfitted temperamentally or technically to deal with the homosexual inside or outside of the confessional, facilities should be available whereby he could refer him to another priest whom he knows to be competent and well-informed. Generally, priests will be able to deal with the majority of cases brought to them in the confessional and outside. In extreme cases, however, it would be of great

---

[1] " The first condition of effective spiritual cure rests in the greeting. It is a very difficult moment for the invert when he faces up to admitting his inversion. The priest must therefore be very understanding, but discreet and considerate, in his first questions, awakening confidence before going on to speak of spiritual remedies. With many patients, the fact of being able to speak about it openly for the first time without seeing the pharisaic look or the look of naive astonishment on the face of his listener is already the beginning of a cure." *New Problems in Medical Ethics*, p. 116.

spiritual help to the homosexual if priests possessing wider experience than the average were at the disposal of their brethren in numbers proportionate to the need.

Whenever possible the ultimate aim of the priest should be to help the homosexual to become normal. But where this is impossible due to the homosexual tendencies being too strongly entrenched, the homosexual, even though he may never be able to rid himself completely of the inclinations themselves, must be taught to avoid their wilful and sinful expression either internally in thought or desire, or externally in action. Where the struggle seems to continue without any apparent success the penitent must be encouraged, and thus despair and despondency are avoided. His sins should not be minimized, but rather his sense of sin in general and the way it hurts God must be deepened. At the same time he must be taught to deepen his sense of God's love and mercy coupled with a firm trust in His never-failing assistance. The priest's first reaction to the homosexual should be an answer tinged with optimism, while at the same time refraining from a pretence of promising a panacea.

The priest must break the fatalism which usually obsesses the homosexual. On the other hand, over-optimism should be avoided. If, when the homosexual is assured that his homosexuality is not fatalistic, he is also informed that his sexual deviation is not difficult to bring under control, there is grave danger that he will lose confidence at the first fall. The priest must point out to him that his physical cure is not instantaneous and that were he to fall in the future this will not mean that God has deserted him or that it is impossible for him to become other than he is. The nature of grace must be explained to him and he must appreciate the influence which habit still exercises over his actions. If the priest neglects to attend to these matters then at his first fall the homosexual may feel left with less hope than before, as previously he believed in the efficacy of the priest's assistance; now he is convinced that there is no hope at all for one in his condition.

One of the first questions he will put before the priest concerns his responsibility for his condition or his actions were he to indulges his tendencies. The priest should not overwhelm the penitent with the heinousness of his sins at his first meeting. He should attempt to strengthen the homosexual's will and enlighten his mind so that he may tell the truth gradually in a frank, open way, so that eventually the extent of his responsibility may be gauged. The homosexual should not be told that he is completely responsible, or that he is in no way responsible: *some liberty, and therefore some responsibility should be presumed.* Later, when the penitent has a greater knowledge of himself and his anomaly, the case will be judged in a fuller light, and the question of responsibility can be re-introduced and finally settled.

The priest is usually consulted by two classes of penitents: those who suspect that they may be homosexual and wish to know the truth, and those who know themselves to be homosexuals and come seeking advice or a cure. Owing to the greater publicity now given to the problem, many otherwise 'confirmed bachelors' may begin to suspect that they are abnormal in the direction of their sexual drive. A man may be perplexed by his lack of interest in the physical relationship of marriage.

He may confess that hitherto he gravitated towards male company, even though sexual acts may never have taken place. Others who have experienced homosexual attractions in the past, to which they may or may not have given expression, will attempt to name their anomaly. Penitents may come to the priest for a variety of reasons: hope of being restored to normality; afraid of yielding to their homosexual desires; ashamed of the social stigma which is attached to homosexuality.

It is very difficult to give a hard and fast rule for distinguishing the homosexual from the heterosexual. The priest should not jump to hasty conclusions, based solely on the presence or absence of homosexual practices. At the same time, these acts are an indication of the subject's sexual bias. If they do occur, and it is generally the practising homosexual who approaches the priest in the confessional, careful enquiry should be made as to the nature, frequency and circumstances of these homosexual acts. This enquiry should be coupled with an examination of the person's attitude to the other sex. Experience will teach the priest to detect the signs that point in one direction or in the other.

The penitent may be conscious of strong homosexual tendencies to which he has never succumbed. Self-discipline, which is so important if the homosexual is to attempt a heterosexual re-orientation, is already present in such a case. Such a person must not be made to feel that temptation in this abnormal form is a sin. The Church does not reject the homosexual who is assailed by homosexual temptation any more than she condemns the normal man tempted heterosexually. Those who fight temptation of any kind are winning the Kingdom of Heaven, and the long painful struggle and constant effort to remain chaste has gained for many souls magnificent spiritual progress. The chaste homosexual is probably largely blameless for his condition—in some cases he certainly is—and his continence gives more favourable indications of successful heterosexualization. He shows far more virtue than the so-called ' he-man ' who does not control his lust, since man's strength is measured by integrity of soul rather than physical characteristics.

## II. THE HOMOSEXUAL

So much for the priest's attitude to the homosexual. But what of the *attitude of the homosexual to the priest*? Ordinarily the homosexual who approaches the priest sincerely desires to become other than he is and there is little difficulty in discovering from his attitude if this is so. But there are other types which should also be recognized should they appear. Just as in other sins, the priest may encounter the person who carries on homosexual practices with no apparent purpose of amendment. Again there is the homosexual who instead of a genuine religious sense, is imbued with *false religiosity*. This false religiosity often accompanies the homosexual condition and since ' religion' does not penetrate further than ritualism, it is of no value in his struggle to fight his homosexual tendencies. In fact it may be a positive hindrance when he seeks ' religion' as an expression of his sexual deviation.

The homosexual, too, is sometimes encountered who approaches the priest in a passing moment of sincerity, or perhaps out of sheer *exhibitionism*. He returns to the scene of his sexual indulgence and cancels his next appointment with his pastoral adviser. In many respects he may be compared to the morphiamaniac who, while he enters a home to undergo a cure, conceals drugs on his person. Such a practising homosexual, enchained in his vice which he rejects and yet desires, must be treated as other victims of bad habit. There is no question of modifying the standards of morality, but such a soul will receive sympathetic treatment to help him on to the path of salvation.

Yet another type comes in *temporary heart-break and despair* when he is deserted by his 'partner', and feeling that he can never go through such an experience again decides that the time has come for him to do something about himself. This emotional crisis in the homosexual's life presents the priest with an opportunity of attempting his conversion. Perhaps he too will cancel his next appointment if he has met another 'partner' in the meantime, but if the priest is sufficiently skilful and sympathetic in showing clearly the futility of his life, such a crisis may well become a turning-point. If the will is strengthened, the purpose of amendment may be made firm and lasting.

The only type of homosexual with whom the priest has any real hope of success is the one who *sincerely wishes to become heterosexual* or at least control his homosexual tendencies. Religion is to this type an integrating and vitalizing factor in the struggle against his sexual deviation. The homosexual realizes that he cannot change himself by his unaided efforts, but is dependent on a Higher Power Who is willing and ready to give all the necessary aids, given the agent's co-operation. He must be encouraged to receive the Sacraments as often as possible. With this supernatural aid he believes he can be different, and then wills to become other than he is. As regards the value of the religious approach in the treatment of homosexuals the British Medical Association's Report states:

"Individuals cannot of course be 'dragooned' into a religious experience and pressure in this direction would defeat its own object. There should, however, be a recognition of the fact that homosexuals can acquire a new direction in their lives through religious conversion, and opportunities should be available to them to discover for themselves a basis of life that proves a reality to many people."[2]

The value of an admission of this kind is enhanced in that it derives from a purely medical source. Previously the Report admitted that some homosexuals "adjust as a result of spiritual experience".[3] Belief in a personal God, who is ready to afford him all supernatural assistance, is essential to the homosexual. The reconciliation of the practising homosexual with God in the Sacrament of Penance is perhaps the priest's easiest task, but there the pastoral work is only beginning. He must so encourage and fortify the penitent that he not only perseveres in his avoidance of future lapses, but ultimately desires normality, the ideal constantly put before him by his confessor.

*The priest must re-educate the homosexual as to the nature of sexuality*, and this re-education involves a completely new approach by the homosexual also in matters not connected with the genital sphere. The homosexual must be inspired with the desire to become a God-centred

[2] *Op cit.*, p. 49.    [3] *Ibid.*, p. 43.

personality, whose main concern in the future is to do God's will and not his own.  In such a way the homosexual will no longer be dominated by his homosexual propensity, nor the need to satisfy its instincts.  He acquires a new passion which is out-going and creative, thus affording him greater satisfaction.  The void in his heart is filled with a new hope and love, replacing the old which hither- to he found so rewarding, if barren, delighting him more than anything else.

The priest has shown him the richness of the charity of Christ, explained the true destiny of man, and indicated how homosexual love was suicidal by its very nature, cut- ting itself off from God and society; the latter he has doubtless realized for himself already, but the former must often be forcibly instilled.  The homosexual should be told that his condition is a misfortune, and that even the most talented homosexual is no more to be envied his homosexuality than the blind man his blindness.  No compensation would repay the happiness of true hetero- sexual love, and the last thing to be desired is to remain homosexual.  However, it is very hard to convince even some chaste homosexuals of this truth.

### III. THE PRIEST AND THE ADOLESCENT

In the homosexual pattern, however, perhaps as in no other sexual problem, prevention is better than cure.  The priest's most important duties include instructing parents as to their great task in rearing their children in a proper moral atmosphere.  He is more directly concerned, how- ever, in dealing with the problem as it manifests itself in the adolescent. What is the best pastoral advice to be given to an adolescent who admits that he has indulged in homosexual practices with a younger boy, another adolescent, or with an adult? Since at adolescence the homosexual is scarcely distinguishable from his heterosexual companions, it is always best to assume that he is not a homosexual. To tell him that he is a homosexual, or in danger of becoming one, may leave an obsessive memory in the highly impressionable adolescent. He may not even have heard of homosexuality, and thus not know what the priest is talking about, in which case he may satisfy his curiosity from unsavoury sources and pick up erroneous ideas. *He should not be made to feel abnormal*, or that he is an irreversibly conditioned homosexual, but treated as any other adolescent at grips with a sexual problem.

He may certainly be told that, unlike solitary sexual sins, he is to some degree co-operating with and tempting another to sin, and thus his sense of chivalry may be appealed to. If there is affection between the parties, the essential difference between friendship and love must be stressed. He may also be told that such habits if persisted in, might well spoil his chances of a happy marriage in later life, an ideal to be kept constantly before him. Even if he does happen to be homosexually conditioned, *he should be encouraged to act normally*, then at least his homosexual propensity will have passed unnoticed by others and he will be able to adapt himself more easily to normal society in adult life.

What is true of other sexual difficulties at adolescence is also true where homosexual acts are concerned. The youth must be treated firmly, and the uselessness of such a practice, resulting in grave personal unhappiness, must be stressed. A positive rather than a negative repressive approach is desirable. He must be taught to train his will, and, except in obvious cases of involuntary acts, it must be emphasized that, though difficult at times, *he must and can restrain himself.* No attempt should be made to minimize the moral guilt, nor on the other hand to stress the emotional guilt. Leniency will weaken his will to fight just as over-severity may drive him to despair.[4] High ideals should be put before him, and above all he must attempt to see his problem in its true proportions. He should realize that this is just a passing phase, and that in later years it will puzzle him that he ever felt that way. Above all he should not take himself too seriously, and *a sense of humour is a great weapon, which he can use to good effect.*[5]

The priest should stress the fact that the adolescent is missing the full life intended for him by God, and that while he may be enjoying the present, he is planting seeds of loneliness and despair for the future. The sentiment of love which is in danger of going astray permanently must be re-educated, and the soul of the adolescent must desire to open itself to the enriching qualities of the giving of self. For the homosexual who wishes to control his tendencies, the late Fr. King has some excellent advice which, however, tends to be too negative in approach:

[4] " There are some psychiatrists who are less lenient in the matter of responsibility than some confessors, precisely because they realize that too much leniency weakens the patient's will to fight." *Psychiatry and Catholicism*, p. 370.

[5] " There is at adolescence an absence of humour about oneself which makes one too willing to believe that one is an example of an unusual and little understood mental peculiarity." Introduction by R. H. Thouless, M.A., Ph.D., *The Invert*, p. xxi.

" 1. Make up your mind clearly that in no case and under no circumstances will you allow your attraction to lead you into wrong behaviour of any kind.

2. Avoid touching the other person in any way which could not be done in the full light of day in public.

3. Treat the other person normally—seek his company just to the same extent as you seek that of others, and no more.

4. Do not markedly avoid him, or act in a strange or conspicuous manner with regard to him.

5. Do not talk or think of the attraction at all. When it recurs to your mind turn at once to some other interesting topic.

6. Get a sufficient amount of fresh air and exercise, and look after your bodily health. Low health, fatigue and worry often make the imagination very unmanageable and treacherous."[6]

The priest may be in charge of *boys in a boarding school* where he discovers that homosexual practices occur between the pupils. He should limit the facilities for the occurrence of such sexual play, and see that the adolescents concerned engage in outdoor games or other interesting distractions, as well as being afforded the opportunity of meeting those of the opposite sex. He should not publicly display the culprits to the school, as generally speaking exclusive friendships of adolescence will break themselves up if they degenerate to genital acts. If the adolescent refuses to forego his homosexual acts, he should be removed from the school as quietly and as quickly as possible. Apart from these disciplinary measures, the priest should act as any other priest would in the spiritual guidance of adolescents.

Since the teaching profession does attract some homosexuals who enter from unworthy motives, some kind of screening or examination should be undertaken which would exclude such immoral men from schoolmastering. This would establish on a firmer basis the trust between child and teacher, and between teacher and parent. As regards this aspect of screening teachers, the British Medical Association's Report states:

"Those associated with the education, training, and activities of youth should be carefully selected. . . . If the morals of the school or institution as a whole is high, any occurence of homosexual activity will not be difficult to handle. . . . More care on the part of those responsible for such appointments would eliminate the risk of presenting excellent opportunities for indulgence to those homosexuals who, consciously or unconsciously, are attracted to work amongst youth just because of its opportunities. . . . At school age the importance of child and parent guidance as a preventive factor becomes clear, and it should be developed, together with parent-teacher associations."[7]

## IV. THE HOMOSEXUAL MILIEU

*The practising homosexual adult* generally gravitates to a homosexual milieu where he feels thoroughly at home with his own kind; where he feels he is understood and enjoys the enormous relief of 'being himself'. The difficulty of a cure for such an individual, either as regards a return to heterosexuality or at least the controlling of his homosexual tendencies, is proportioned in almost every case to the extent of his fixation in his homosexual milieu. There are cases, however, where the homosexual

[7] *Homosexuality and Prostitution*, pp. 41-2.

despises his fellow-homosexuals, refusing to mix with them at any level because he dreads their discovering his homosexual bias. Even if he lapses with varying frequency into homosexual acts, his attitude of mind may give greater hope for recovery and re-orientation.

Yet to shun the homosexual milieu and seek a new and healthier heterosexual one may well be the most difficult decision the homosexual has to make, since the attractive nature of his surroundings has probably been one of the chief factors in the growth of his homosexual propensity. Lonely in the company of other men where he feels a misfit, he discovers friendship and understanding in a homosexual milieu. There are not infrequent cases where there is question of a gifted nature whose intellectual or artistic qualities have found stimulation among other homosexuals of the same type. Wherever this *intellectual and aesthetic aspect of homosexuality* is discovered, the priest should attempt the spiritual re-education of thought and sentiment of the homosexual, and help him to appreciate that this enriching aspect of his anomaly is a clumsy concealing of what is in effect a fundamental denial of authentic human values. False appearances must be dismissed, even though the homosexual may feel that he can corroborate the enriching value of homosexuality from his own personal experience.

His temperament and possibly poor character training, which may have led him into a homosexual milieu, will now impede his retracing his steps. Without his homosexual friends he finds the world an empty void, and in a moment of weakness he may slip back once more into his vice. He may well have to defend himself against the solicitations of his old friends, who may not intend to renew overt relationships but desire merely to cling to the would-be reformer. They pursue him as the lover pursues his beloved.

He needs good friends of the same sex with whom, if he is a practising homosexual, there is no danger of physical relationships occurring. He can relax in their company, and perhaps gradually assume their approach to sexual matters. However, close single friendships are to be avoided, and the larger and more varied his circle of friends the more beneficial will be the results. The homosexual seems to have a need and *desire for exclusive friendships*, but this must be strongly discouraged by the priest. He should be welcomed into good Christian families where he feels he belongs, and where his natural love of children, so common among homosexuals, should provide a strong incentive to achieve heterosexuality and family life for himself. He must also be helped to find his place in a Christian community where he can play an active part in its charitable and social work.

Most homosexuals are not averse to *the society of women*, yet avoid close specific attachments which would lead to the intrusion of matrimonial prospects from a mis-interpretation of their friendship. Homosexuals them-selves are often to blame on this account. However, certain types of women who attract, and are attracted by homosexuals should in general be avoided. There is, for instance, the woman who regards the homosexual as a sister with whom she may engage in female chatter, and from whom she believes she gets more sympathy and under-standing than she would from normal men friends. There is the added benefit of having a male escort in public whom she knows will make no further demands on her. Homosexuals too should avoid associating too frequently with older women, since this may well take the form of a mother-substitute due to a faulty early environment. Usually, however, the friendship is offered for its own sake where the homosexuals feel that no misunderstanding over marriage can possibly arise.   Any friendships with women, provided they are at all suitable, are to be strongly encouraged as contributing materially to their adjustment, and eventually the homosexual may meet a sufficiently suitable member of the opposite sex with whom he may contemplate marriage.

However, the homosexual must be warned that his greatest danger comes from within himself.  He must be braced against those insidious and destructive emotions so characteristic of the homosexual pattern—*self-pity*, and a strong tendency towards morbid introspection.  All the advice which we have given so far are aids to dispel the loneliness which seems the characteristic trait of the homosexual, who also possesses an overpowering desire for sympathy.  If he lacks these he may be driven to imprudent confidences which may prove later not only a source of embarrassment, but also encourage unsuitable friendships. The confessor should warn the homosexual against becoming involved, however slightly, in any strata of homosexual society, or associating too closely with other known homosexuals. This would tend to ostracize him from the normal type of society which is best suited to help him.  He should be advised against indulging in all forms of escapism which would retard his sexual re-orientation, and strive to appear as normal as possible, shunning all eccentricities of dress or manner.  Discretion about his homosexual tendencies is of the utmost importance.

'Anomaly' has some excellent practical points of advice for the homosexual:

"Don't commit to writing any admission as to your inclinations; don't masquerade—on any occasion whatsoever —in women's clothes, take female parts in theatrical performances, or use make-up; don't be too meticulous in the matter of your clothes, or affect extremes in colour or cut; don't wear conspicuous rings, watches, cufflinks or other jewellery; don't allow your voice or intonation to display feminine inflection—cultivate a masculine tone and method of expression—don't stand with your hand on your hip, or walk mincingly; don't become identified with the groups of inverts which form in every city; don't let it be noticed that you are bored by female society; don't persuade yourself into believing that love is the same thing as friendship; don't become involved in marked intimacies with men who are not of your own age or set; don't let your enthusiasm for particular male friends make you conspicuous in their eyes, or in the eyes of society; don't occupy yourself with work or pastimes which are distinctly feminine; don't, under any circumstances, compromise yourself by word or action with strangers."[8]

On the positive side, he adds:

"Hold frank conversations with suitable persons, thereby avoiding mental repression; encourage every symptom of sexual normalization; cultivate self-esteem; become deeply engrossed in a congenial occupation or hobby; observe discretion and practise self-restraint."[9]

[8] The Invert, pp. 135-6.
[9] Ibid., p. 137.

O

CHAPTER TWELVE

# Treatment and Future of the Homosexual

~~~~~~~~~~~~~~~~~~~~~~~~~~~~~~~~~~~~~~~~~~~~~~~~~~~~~~~~~~~

## I. TREATMENT

THE aim of all pastoral care of the homosexual should be ultimately his re-orientation to heterosexuality and where this is impossible an adjustment to his condition in the only way acceptable to Catholic moral theology—a life of chastity. The treatment of the homosexual is still very much an open question among doctors and psychiatrists, and until recently both were in agreement in excluding the priest from taking part in the therapy they thought necessary. These days there has been a definite change of attitude, and the inference underlying the British Medical Association's Report is that many doctors would find a priest's influence helpful to a solution of their therapeutic problems. Nowadays, it is not so unusual for a psychiatrist to enlist the aid of a well-informed priest in the achievement of the essential element in any psychiatric treatment—that the homosexual should desire to be cured of his condition. The former attitude, of course, was by no means all the fault of the lay specialists. Some priests seem still unreasonably opposed to any interference from outside in what they consider an exclusively moral problem, while others wrongly hold that they have nothing to offer the homosexual in his desire to become heterosexual. Some of the latter class even minimize the assistance they can offer in helping the gravely-tempted homosexual to control his tendencies. Yet it must be obvious that just as the medical and psychiatric treatments are not mutually exclusive, so it is equally necessary not to exclude the ministry of the priest even at this purely natural level. The priest has a very important contribution to make.

There will be many cases where the priest cannot work alone, and he too must enlist the help of doctor or psychiatrist. Drugs, as we have seen, are useful as a temporary measure to relieve anxiety in a small number of homosexuals who are highly sexed, seriously tempted, and despair of ever gaining control over the expression of their deviate tendencies. With the aid of these drugs, such homosexuals are in a better position to break the vicious circle of their sexual practices. Psychiatric treatment is beneficial also where the individual is suffering from advanced anxiety states, or other psychological disorders.

We believe the numbers and proportion of homosexuals needing medical or psychiatric care has been grossly exaggerated in the past. Yet we have no reason to doubt the sincerity of doctors or psychiatrists when they press their respective claims, for, generally speaking, only extreme cases of homosexuality come their way. Furthermore the majority of these cases originate in physical or psychical disorders not necessarily related to homosexuality. Unless these facts are borne in mind, the doctor or psychiatrist may easily arrive at a false diagnosis.

The priest, on his part, cannot ignore any legitimate aid which will enable any of his faithful to overcome their homosexual tendencies or indulgences. When the priest collaborates with the doctor or psychiatrist so that their work is complementary then the most favourable circumstances are being established for the spiritual and physical well-being of the homosexual. The choice of a Christian psychiatrist is a delicate matter since many prescribed psychiatric methods of homosexual therapy are in direct opposition to the Church's moral teaching. These methods often ignore the fundamental principles of man's nature and his supernatural destiny. Yet priests have been known to thwart delicate cures by their ignorance of basic medical and psychiatric therapeutic techniques. Therefore we believe that facilities should be made available whereby an exchange of views and principles could be effected between the parties concerned.

Some psychiatrists, for example, in their treatment of neurosis, speak of the crucial moment of enlightenment when the subject sees himself as he is. It is the moment when he realizes the true nature of his disorder, and begins to understand the foolishness and destructiveness of his behaviour, as well as the motives which brought it about. Psychiatrists demand his acceptance of the uncomplimentary truth about himself as a necessary therapeutic measure, since without this adequate self-knowledge of the cause of his inner conflicts the patient cannot even begin the journey back to mental health. The priest finds a parallel in the story of the conversion of St. Augustine. A long series of graces had brought him to the state analogous to the psychiatric 'moment of realization' where he saw clearly what he was, what he ought to be, and what steps he must take in order to change.

Conversion, however, entails more than a mere act of the will.[1] Without a re-appraisal of his world in the light of supernatural values, the homosexual will be unable to ensure a real and lasting change of heart. He needs to have faith that God will give him the light to understand his own disorder. Grace is not magic, but it is sufficient for any man to withstand formal grave sin, and this is as true for him as for any other sinner. Given his good-will, courage and resolution, the homosexual can, with the grace of God, gradually, perhaps almost imperceptibly, transform his own personality. However, he must not presume upon its sufficiency without his own conscious and persevering co-operation.

Indirectly prayer and the Sacraments do confirm natural therapy in so far as they elevate the homosexual to his supernatural destiny, and buttress his will with the resolution to overcome future temptations however violent their character. His cure, whether it be heterosexualization or the controlling of his tendencies, may well entail years of self-denial with personal discipline as the dominant note. By supernatural help he becomes ready and willing to do whatever is God's will for him. His will, strengthened by a singleness of purpose and clarity of aim, knows what it wants and pursues it with all its energy. The most important factor of his conversion lies in his desire to be

---

[1] " Through conversion there is a complete upheaval and redirection of the emotional life of the individual. Conversion not only re-orientates the imagination and the whole mode of living, but cures, for example, various forms of neurosis, alcoholism, or anti-social behaviour. In losing his self-centredness the individual not only becomes free from such emotions as fear, guilt and resentment, but free from the grip of indulgence. Conversion gives the subject a personal faith that God can satisfy his deepest needs." *Homosexuality and Prostitution*, p. 90.

free from his anomaly which hitherto he thought could never be overcome.

What are the chances of success in the treatment of homosexuals? Is the condition so ingrained in the majority of cases that natural therapy must confine itself to merely helping the homosexual to avoid homosexual practices, or is it generally possible to re-direct his sexual drive into heterosexual channels? To classify the condition as always either completely curable or incurable, dependent on whether or not it is essential or acquired, is a grave mistake. Some doctors make all homosexuality essential, and further claim that it cannot be cured. Moralists, on the other hand, have tended to regard the homosexual as one who could really change his condition if he so desired, since they consider all homosexuality to be completely acquired. But in every group of homosexuals, whether acquired or essential, one will find that some are curable while others seem irreversibly fixed in their deviation. It is an accepted fact too that even where there seems to be a very strong constitutional element present, one generally discovers that environmental factors and habit have also entered into the strengthening of the deviation. However, where the condition has been acquired there are brighter hopes of heterosexualization, all depending on what is the overall personality of the patient, and to what extent he has indulged himself in the past. It is an accepted fact that many acquired homosexuals cure themselves of the habit without having recourse to either doctor or psychiatrist, and therefore do not influence the judgements of the latter, which are in the main rather pessimistic. Yet even when the condition appears to be innately determined all possibility of success cannot be *a priori* excluded.

An examination of psychiatric results in this field affords a much more hopeful prospect of complete success than that allowed in medical circles. Psychiatrists, however, demand as necessary conditions for any effective treatment that the patient be young, anxious to be treated, and the condition itself not too deeply ingrained. The most strikingly optimistic document of recent times was written by Dr. Hadfield who claims that his patients were completely cured of their homosexual propensities to the extent of leading normal heterosexual lives.[2] He attacks the late Havelock Ellis's theory that all homosexuality is constitutionally determined, and disclosed that the latter admitted to him that his sole reason for holding such a view was his desire to exonerate the homosexual from all blame. However, as we have said, the question of treatment is still wide open and we welcome future investigations in this sphere of the homosexual problem.

## II. THE HOMOSEXUAL'S FUTURE

Some priests, such as Dom Moore, for example, hold that the homosexual can overcome his homosexual propensity and embrace *the married state*.[3] But the evidence suggests that, except in individual cases, marriage is no cure for the homosexual. One exception might be that of the homosexual who is also strongly attached sexually to the opposite sex. A happy marriage in his case could

---

[2] 'The Cure of Homosexuality.' *British Medical Journal*, (June 7th, 1958) pp. 1323-6. J. A. Hadfield, M.B., Ch.B. Lecturer on Psychopathology and Mental Hygiene, University of London.

[3] 'The Pathogenesis and Treatment of Homosexual Disorders.' *Journal of Personality*, XIV (September 1945) p. 72. Thomas V. Moore, O.S.B.

prove an efficacious remedy against the deviate side of his psycho-sexual life, since it would tend to develop his heterosexual tendencies with a consequent diminishing of the homosexual.  But in such instances each individual case should be carefully considered in its varying circumstances, and a judgement given accordingly.  Unfortunately we know relatively little of the general effect of marriage on homosexuals.  Those who lack any erotic attraction towards those of the opposite sex, and are even sometimes repelled by them, can scarcely be expected to find happiness in marriage.

The wife, in such circumstances, would be exposed to a parody of homosexual relations as she might well be requested to perform the same kind of unnatural acts that her husband would perform with one of his own sex. In any case she would be denied his full affection.  Unfortunately there are some priests who imagine that once the homosexual has experienced normal marital relationships he will lose all his homosexual desires.  Yet women who marry homosexuals on that presupposition are often subjected to a cruel awakening.  It must be remembered that the homosexual of strong homosexual tendencies is bound to inform his future wife of his deviate inclinations.

Where there is little likelihood of marriage, the priest must seriously consider counselling the homosexual as to his *choice of life in a celibate setting*.  It is an undeniable phenomenon of homosexuality that there is a tendency, whether conscious or otherwise, for the homosexual to gravitate towards those professions and activities where he can be in constant contact with men or youths.  The priest must warn the homosexual, who has not learned to sublimate and control his tendencies, that schoolmastering, scouting and the like must be avoided generally as dangerous occasions of sin. He may well protest his special qualities for such work, but an affirmative judgement cannot be given except after the most intensive inquiries. However, there are cases where the chaste homosexual may be allowed to take up such work. But as there have been so many unfortunate results in the past, the most prudent course to adopt would be to refuse consent until the contrary is positively proved beyond all shadow of doubt. In such a grave matter the priest should err on the side of severity rather than clemency.

A much more difficult problem is whether the homosexual may offer himself as a candidate for *the priesthood*. Throughout her long history the Church has been slow to regard the homosexual as a suitable candidate, even though he may be richly gifted with those personal qualities of intelligence and character that may urge his acceptance. Indeed, one may apodictically say that the general rule is to deny the possibility of the priesthood to the homosexual, especially to those in whom the deviation predominates, and even more to those who have indulged their tendencies in homosexual practices. Furthermore, it must also be refused those whose desire for the priesthood is an escape from the feared consequences of a complete cure—the married state—so that their celibacy is merely the effect of a previous refusal to accept women on the psycho-sexual plane. The state of virginity has no supernatural value unless it is embraced for the Kingdom of Christ, and therefore, to embrace a life of chastity out of exaggerated self-interest, pride, or a desire to shun the burdens of married life, is not to embrace the Christian virtue.

An interesting paper on vocations, reporting the conclusions of a conference of priests and doctors in Belgium, is presented by Father Roger Troisfontaines in the *Nouvelle Revue Theologique*: 'A propos de la vocation sacerdotale: Indications et contre-indications'.[4] He enumerated among the absolute contra-indications, mental weakness shown by false reasoning, feelings of superiority or persecution and any indications of paranoia. Even though sex deviations are contra-indications, says Father Troisfontaines, they are not absolute, but "at least two years of probation outside the seminary or religious house should be imposed, to see whether, with the help of proper psychotherapy, normal reactions will replace the perverse tendencies".[5]

As a general rule, therefore, we hold that the priest should be extremely reluctant to advise the homosexual to contemplate embracing the sacerdotal state. This is not to say that from a theoretical view there can be no exceptions. Practically speaking, however, homosexuality is a bar to the priesthood. If a homosexual were ever to be considered as a candidate for the priesthood then a very careful and scrutinizing inquiry should be made of the motives which move him to seek this exalted way of life. Any kind of homosexual practice, or indeed a pronounced propensity in his conduct, would be a bar to his acceptance. One might possibly make an exception to conduct confined to adolescence, but even in this case there is room for hesitation, and especial regard should be paid to the nature of the practices, and the speed with which he forsook them.

[4] *Op. cit.*, 76 (July-August, 1954) pp. 716-21.
[5] *Ibid.*, p. 721.

It must also be remembered that the priestly life of celibacy is often attractive to the homosexual and he may desire to embrace it. But the desire for the priesthood is not enough in itself. It must be accompanied by the certain knowledge of one's capacity for perfect chastity based on one's conduct in the past. The priesthood or religious life should never be recommended as states for getting rid of bad-habits, or be regarded as vocations in which the capacity for chastity is acquired. The late Holy Father, Pope Pius XII, has urged those responsible to run no risks when they examine prospective candidates. If they have any serious doubts as to the possibility of these being unable to keep perfect chastity, then they should use their authority to get them to give up their vocation.[6] If the candidate's past attempts at chastity have been unhappy, then they should not scruple to refuse his request. There is no room for doubt that a candidate who has contracted evil habits of a homosexual nature, which he has not overcome by the time he enters a major seminary, should be told to leave.

However, if it is finally settled that the candidate may go forward for the priesthood a very important question to be decided is *the choice of secular or regular clergy*, apostolic or contemplative life. Father Larère favours the religious life because the secular priest lacks the framework of the cloister.[7] Yet in general terms it would seem that the activity of the secular priest's life is such as to afford less time for indulging in self-pity. In his daily work the priest will meet other souls less fortunate than

[6] De Sacra Virginitate, March 25th, 1954. *Acta Apostolicae Sedis*, XLVI (May 16th, 1954) pp. 161-91.
[7] *New Problems in Medical Ethics*, p. 122.

himself who are struggling for perfection, and he will give them the necessary sympathy because he has known what it is to conquer temptation in himself. The monastic life on the other hand may give too much time for introspection, and because of the strictly male environment, afford more dangerous occasions of sin. Each individual case should be examined, but, in general, the secular clergy should be the first consideration put before the candidate.

# Conclusion

~~~~~~~~~~~~~~~~~~~~~~~~~~~~~~~~~~~~~~~~~~~~~~~~~~~~~~~~~~~~~~

HOMOSEXUALITY is not a disease. The hormonal theory has been so exploded by recent medical experiments that it is being speedily jettisoned by its former devotees. The homosexual in general is not inexorably determined by heredity or his own physical condition. It is to be regretted that most therapeutic measures in the past have confined themselves to helping the homosexual to keep his tendencies under control. We do not accept this fatalism which has wrought such havoc in perpetuating the homosexual's conviction that his deviation is stronger than he is, and that he can do nothing about it. It is certainly not too sanguine to look forward to a new era in which the medical stress will be directed to formulating *positive* measures designed to assist the homosexual in his attempts to lead *a normal heterosexual life*. The homosexual can *become normal*, and while we are aware that there is little available information concerning the treatment of homosexuals, everything is to be gained from this optimistic attitude which will soon transmit itself to the homosexual patient.

Homosexuality is an unnatural condition, and the homosexual is generally in varying degrees responsible for its origin, and even more for its expression in homosexual practices. But where there is responsibility there is also hope. The Church throughout the ages condemned homosexual practices and many present-day writers, attacking her abstract morality, accuse her of being unrealistic in so far as she ignores modern scientific progress in diagnosing homosexuality. The 'condition', they say, was unknown to the early Church and now she must change her laws and adapt them to the 'new science'. Yet the Church is still performing today, as she did through the centuries, her mission of leading all men to God. Religion and all it has to offer is one of the most effective factors in the homosexual's re-habilitation. The priest, no longer deterred by the false claim that homosexuality is essentially a medical or psychiatric problem, must enter the field and spread the truth. He must assist the homosexual to beg God's healing and elevating grace so that he may take his rightful place in Christian society. Modern scientific theories are but mists which some moralists use in their attempts to obscure the teaching of the True Church. But we find that on closer examination these mists disappear leaving the old altars standing.

APPENDIX

# The Catholic and Homosexual Penal Reform

~~~~~~~~~~~~~~~~~~~~~~~~~~~~~~~~~~~~~~~~

THE following statement was published in the *Westminster Cathedral Chronicle*:

*"In view of the enquiries which have reached Archbishop's House following the publication of the report of the Home Office Departmental Committee on prostitution and homosexuality, His Grace the Archbishop of Westminster has thought it useful to set forth the following principles which should be borne in mind when consideration is given to the proposals regarding homosexual acts between consenting adults:*

The civil law takes cognizance primarily of public acts. Private acts *as such* are outside its scope.

However, there are certain private acts which have public consequence in so far as they affect the common good. These acts may rightly be subject to civil law.

It may be, however, that the civil law cannot effectively control such acts without doing more harm to the common good than the acts themselves would do. In that case it may be necessary in the interests of the common good to tolerate without approving such acts.

It has, for example, invariably been found that adultery or fornication (which, however private, have clear public consequences) cannot effectively be controlled by civil law without provoking greater evils.

197

Applying these principles to the question of homosexual acts between consenting males:

1. As regards the moral *law*, Catholic moral teaching is:

(I) *Homosexual acts are grievously sinful.*

(II) That in view of the public consequences of these acts, e.g., the harm which would result to the common good if homosexual conduct became widespread or an accepted mode of conduct in the public mind, the civil law does not exceed its legitimate scope if it attempts to control them by making them crimes.

The teaching authority of the Bishops is primarily concerned with laying down these two principles of *law* which cannot be denied by any Catholic.

2. However, two questions of *fact* arise:

(I) If the law takes cognizance of private acts of homosexuality and makes them crimes, do worse evils follow for the common good?

(II) Since homosexual acts between consenting males are now crimes in law, would a change in the law harm the common good by seeming to condone homosexual conduct?

Ecclesiastical authority could rightly give a decision on this question of fact as well as on the question of the moral law, if the answers to questions of fact were overwhelmingly clear. As, however, various answers are possible in the opinion of prudent men, Catholics are free to make up their own minds on these two questions of fact."

## OUR VIEW

To the first question of fact we answer in the negative since it is our firm conviction that as matters stand in England today one of the greatest preventives of homosexuality is the legal condemnation of society. It is the law and not science that holds society together, and before any legal change may be even contemplated a further enlightenment on the subject is necessary together with a strengthening of the moral fibre of the nation. Of course, we willingly admit that the attempt to suppress homosexual activity by law is only one factor in diminishing the problem as a whole. That is why in chapter six of this book we have stressed the importance of a good Christian family which would enable the individual to lead a morally healthy life. The British Medical Association's Report holds very much the same view: "A public opinion against homosexual practices is a greater safeguard [than legal sanction], and this can be achieved by promoting in the minds, motives and wills of the people a desire for clean and unselfish living."[1] We are alarmed at the growing complacency with which some people nowadays regard homosexual practices, and the repealing of the existing law would be ill-advised and might well have disastrous results. The individual must appreciate his position in society, and if he has little time for its accepted code then he must accept the consequences. He must learn self-discipline and unselfishness, and we do not feel that this would be achieved by weakening still further the already weak structure of society.

As to the second question of fact, we feel that there has been a DEFINITE LINK between crime and sin, and thus if the law were repealed the conclusion drawn by many modern writers on the subject would be to equate penal reform and a new 'existentialist morality'. Sympathy with the personal problem of the individual homosexual must never blind a true Christian to the fact that homosexuality, whether of condition or activity, is unnatural.

[1] *Op cit.*, p. 10.

# Medical Terms

~~~~~~~~~~~~~~~~~~~~~~~~~~~~~~~~~~~~~~~~~~~~~~~~~

*Androgen.* Male sex hormone which directly produces masculine characteristics.

*Chromosome.* One of the several microscopic rod-like bodies which appear in cell nuclei at the time of cell division or mitosis. They carry genes which are responsible for transmission of the cell's characteristics and hence those of the individual. The number of chromosomes is constant for a species. They are seen only on special staining.

*Endocrine.* Applied to glands which secrete internally in the bloodstream e.g. adrenal glands and sex glands, as opposed to the salivary glands which secrete externally into the mouth.

*Eunuchism.* The condition of the castrated male.

*Eunuchoidism.* The defective state of the testicles and particularly their dysfunction.

*Gene.* A physical body, part of the chromosome, which transmits characteristics and traits from cell to cell and from individual to individual i.e. they are the ultimate physical units in the inheritance of physical characteristics.

*Hormone.* A chemical substance produced in one organ which is transported by the bloodstream to produce an effect in another organ e.g. adrenal producing blanching of the skin and quickening of the heart when one is frightened.

*Gonadotropin.* A hormone usually produced by the anterior pituitary gland in the brain, or by the placenta. These hormones stimulate, *inter alia*, the testes (or ovaries) and so help to co-ordinate sex gland function. They are Indirect Sex Hormones.

*Intermitotic Nuclei.* Ordinary division of a cell or mitosis has several stages during which the cell's nucleus's chromosomes appear. They change their shape and arrangement and so present characteristic appearances of intermitotic nuclei. This 'dance of the chromosomes' ensures that the two new cells have the same characteristics as their parent cell (see chromosome).

*Oestrogen.* Female sex hormone which directly produces female characteristics.

*Prostate Gland.* Part of the male sex gland system. It sits below the bladder and astride the urethra. Enlargement in the elderly gives difficulty in passing water. It probably produces sex hormones and contributes directly to the preparation of the ejaculate of semen.

*Skin-Biopsy Tests.* Bits of skin are cut off and specially prepared and stained for skilled microscopical examination.

*Stilboestrol.* An artificially produced cheap oestrogen which can be given orally. It is widely used in gynaecology and endocrine disorders.

*Suprarenal Glands.* Endocrine glands which produce effects 'at a distance' by means of hormones which they secrete.  They lie between the kidneys and the lungs.

*Testosterone Propionate.*  As now used, it is an artificially produced male sex hormone suitable for injection and implantation.  It is used for male endocrine disorders e.g. eunuchoidism.


*Note on the Production of Sex Hormones.*  This is carefully balanced by a series of checks and counter-checks. Thus in the development of the male, the anterior pituitary gland produces gonadotropins which stimulate the interstitial or hormone-producing cells of the testis, so that testosterone is freed into the bloodstream.  This helps to produce sexual maturity e.g. breaking of the voice; male body-build; etc: but it tends to inhibit the anterior pituitary's production of gonadotropins.  To what extent the anterior pituitary gland is affected by nervous stimulation from the brain is still debated.

# Bibliography

~~~~~~~~~~~~~~~~~~~~~~~~~~~~~~~~~~~~~~~~~~~~~

ALLEN, C. *Sexual Perversions and Abnormalities*. London, 1949.

"ANOMALY". *The Invert*. London, 1948. 2nd Edition.

ARMSTRONG, C. N., "Diversities of Sex." *British Medical Journal*. I (1955) 1173-1177.

BALLERINI, A., *Opus Theologicum Morale*. Prati, 1890. Vol. I.

BARAHAL, H. S., "Testosterone in Psychotic Male Homosexuals." *Psychiatric Quarterly*. 14 (1940) 319-330.

BARR, M. L., and HOBBS, G. E., "Chromosomal Sex In Transvestites." *Lancet*, I (1954) 1109-1110.

BAILEY, D., *Homosexuality and the Western Christian Tradition*. London, 1955.

——, *Sexual Offenders and Social Punishment*. London, 1956.

*Bible De Jerusalem*. Paris, 1953.

*Bible, La Sainte*. Paris, 1953.

*Bible, The Holy*. Douay Version. London, 1914.

*Bible, The Interpreter's*. New York, 1952.

BRITISH MEDICAL ASSOCIATION AND MAGISTRATES' ASSOCIATION. *The Criminal Law and Sexual Offenders*. London, 1949.

BRITISH MEDICAL ASSOCIATION. *Homosexuality and Prostitution*. London, 1955.

BROWN, F. W., "Heredity in Psychoneuroses." *Proceedings of the Royal Society of Medicine.* 35 (1942) 785-790.

"CANDIDUS". *The Nature of Man: The Problem of Homosexuality.* Cambridge, 1954.

CARPENTER, E., *The Intermediate Sex.* London, 1908.

*Catholic Commentary on Holy Scripture.* London, 1952.

COLE, W. G., *Sex in Christianity and Psycho-Analysis.* London, 1917.

CORY, D. W., *The Homosexual Outlook: A Subjective Approach.* London, 1953.

CURRAN, D., and PARR, D., "Homosexuality; an Analysis of 100 male cases seen in private practice." *British Medical Journal* (April, 1957), 797-801.

DARKE, R. S., "Heredity as an etiological factor in Homosexuality." *Journal of Nervous and Mental Diseases.* 107 (1948), 251-268.

EAST, N., and HUBERT, W., *Psychological Treatment of Crime.* London, 1939.

ELLIS, HAVELOCK. *The Psychology of Sex.* New York, 1956. 3rd Edition.

ESTIUS, *Pauli Epistolae*, VII. Paris, 1844.

FISHMAN, J. F., *Sex in Prison.* New York, 1934.

FORD, D., *The Delinquent Child.* London, 1957.

GENCOUX, J., "Literary Psychoanalysis from Plato to Gide." *New Problems in Medical Ethics.* Cork (1955) 90-107. 1st Series.

GIDE, ANDRÉ, *Corydon: Four Socratic Dialogues.* London, 1952.

GLASS, S. J., DUEL, H. J., and WRIGHT, C. A., "Sex Hormone Studies in Male Homosexuals." *Endocrinology.* 26 (1940) 590-594.

GLEASON, R. W., "Homosexuality: Moral Aspects of the Problem." *Homiletic and Pastoral Review.* (December 1957) 272-278.

GRAVESON, R. H., and CRANE, F. R., *1857-1957. A Century of Family Law.* London, 1957.

HADFIELD, J. A., "The Cure of Homosexuality." *The British Medical Journal,* (June, 1958), 1323-1326.

HARLAND, J. P., "Sodom and Gomorrah." *The Biblical Archaeologist,* VI, 3. 41-54.

HARVEY, J. F., "Homosexuality as a Pastoral Problem." *Theological Studies.* (March, 1955), 86-108.

HEALY, EDWIN F., *Medical Ethics.* Chicago, 1956.

HEFELE, C. J., *Histoire des Conciles.* Paris, 1869.

HEMPHILL, LEITCH and STUART, "A Factual Study of the Male Homosexual Problem." *The British Medical Journal,* (June, 1958), 1317-1323.

HENRY, G. W., *Sex Variants.* New York, 1948.

HIRSCHFELD, M., *Sex Anomalies and Perversions.* London, 1937.

HIRSCHFELD, M., *Sex Pathology.* New York, 1940.

HOME OFFICE. "Report of the Committee on Homosexual Offences and Prostitution." *The Wolfenden Report.* Her Majesty's Stationery Office (Cmnd. 247) (1957).

JACOBI, J., *The Psychology of C. G. Jung.* London, 1951.

JUNG, C. G., *Contributions to Analytical Psychology.* London, 1928.

KALLMAN, F. J., "Comparative Twin Study of the Genetic Aspects of Male Homosexuality." *Journal of Nervous and Mental Diseases.* 115 (1952) 283-298.

KARDINER, A., *Sex and Morality.* London, 1955.

KING, L., S.J., *Sex Enlightenment and the Catholic.*
Bellarmine Series 10, (1947).

KINSEY, A. C., et al. *Sexual Behaviour in the Human Male.* Philadelphia, 1948.

KOLB, L., and JOHNSON, A., "Etiology and Therapy of Overt Homosexuality." *Psychoanalytic Quarterly,* XXIV No. 4. 506-515.

KRAFFT-EBING, R., *Psychopathia Sexualis.* London, 1939. (Trans. of 12th Ed.)

LANG, T., "Studies on the genetic determination of Homosexuality." *Journal of Nervous and Mental Diseases.* 92 (1940) 55 ff.

LEHMKUHL, A., S.J., *Theologia Moralis.* Friburg, 1885. Vol. I, II.

LARERE, PERE CHARLES, "The Passage of the Angel through Sodom." *New Problems in Medical Ethics.* Cork. (1955) 108-123 1st series.

LE MOAL, DR. PAUL, "The Psychiatrist and the Homosexual." *New Problems in Medical Ethics.* Cork, (1955) 70-89 1st series.

LEWIS, C. S., *Surprised by Joy: the Shape of My Early Life.* London, 1955.

LIEBMANN, S., "Homosexuality, Transvestism and Psychosis." *Journal of Nervous and Mental Diseases.* 99 (1944) 945-958.

LURIE, L. A., "The Endocrine Factor in Homosexuality." *American Journal of Medical Science.* 208 (1944) 176-186.

MANSI, J. D., *Sanctorum Conciliorum nova et amplissima collectio.* Florentiae et Venetiis, 1759-1798.

MIGNE. *Patrologia Graeca.*
        *Patrologia Latina.*

MOORE, T. V., "Pathogenesis and Treatment of Homosexual Disorders: a Digest of some Pertinent Evidence." *Journal of Personality.* 14 (1945) 47-83.

MORAN, HERBET M., *In My Fashion.* London, 1946.

MYERSON and NEUSTADT, "Bisexuality and Male Homosexuality." *Clinic,* I (1942) 952-957.

NEUSTADT, R., and MYERSON, A., "Quantitative Sex Hormones Studies in Homosexuality, Childhood and various Neuropsychiatric Disturbances." *American Journal of Psychiatry.* 97 (1940) 524-551.

ODENWALD, ROBERT, "Counselling the Homosexual." *The Priest,* IX (1953).

OWENSBY, N. M., "Homosexuality and Lesbianism treated with Matrazol." *Journal of Nervous and Mental Diseases.* 92 (1940) 65-66.

*Penitentiale Romanum* (ed. Antoninus Augustinus, opera omnia) Lucca, 1767.

PHARR, CLYDE, *The Theodosian Code.* Princeton, 1952.

POLANI, P. E., HUNTER, W. F., and LENNOX, B., "Chromosomal Sex in Turner's Syndrome with Coarctation of the Aorta." *Lancet,* 2 (1954) 120-121.

*Practitioner,* "Sex and its Problems." London (April, 1954).

RADZINOWICZ, DR. L., *Sexual Offences.* Cambridge, 1957.

REES, His Honour Judge TUDOR, and USILL, H. V., *They Stand Apart.* London, 1955.

ROSENWEIG, S., and HOPKINS, R., "A Note on the Ineffectualness of Sex-Hormone Medication in a Case of Pronounced Homosexuality." *Psychosomatic Medicine,* 3 (1941) 87-89.

SANCTI ALPHONSI MARIAE DE LIGORIO. *Theologia Moralis.* Rome, 1905. Tom. I.

SCHWARZ, OSWALD, *The Psychology of Sex*. Reprinted 1956. Pelican Books A.194.

SCOTTISH HOME DEPARTMENT, *Psycho-Therapeutic Treatment of Certain Offenders*. His Majesty's Stationery Office. Edinburgh, 1948.

SLATER, E., "A Demographic Study of a Psychopathic Population." *Annals of Eugenics*. 12 (1944) 121-137.

STRECKER, E. A., *Their Mothers' Sons*. Philadelphia. 1946.

SWYER, G. I. M., "Homosexuality: the Endocrinological Aspects." *The Practitioner*. 172 (April, 1954) 374-377.

TAYLOR, F. H., "Homosexual Offences and their Relation to Psychotherapy." *British Medical Journal*. 2, (1947) 525 ff.

VANN, G., O.P., "Anomalies and Grace." *Blackfriars*. (Oct. 1953) 424-433.

VERMEERSCH, A., S.J., *Theologia Moralis*. Rome, 1922. Tom. I.

VANDERVELDT, J. H., and ODENWALD, R. P., *Psychiatry and Catholicism*. New York, 1952.

WASSERNSCHLEBEN, F., *Die Bussordungen der abendländischen Kirche*. Halle, 1851.

WALKER, K., and STRAUSS, E. B., *Sexual Disorders in the Male*. London, 1948. 3rd Edition.

WESTWOOD, G. W., *Society and the Homosexual*. London, 1952.

# Index of Names

~~~~~~~~~~~~~~~~~~~~~~~~~~~~~~~~~~~~~~~~~~~~~~~~~~~

*Main references are given in bold type*

209

# Index of Subjects

~~~~~~~~~~~~~~~~~~~~~~~~~~~~~~~~~~~~~~~~~~~~~~~~~

*Main references are given in bold type*

211